She Stands in the Storms of Love

Josie West

DEDICATION

To every woman or person who has loved and lost, may this book give you the assurance that you are not alone in your journey. It is my hope that while reading these life experiences of other women that you will find the comfort and peace to know that you are beautiful and deserving of love each in your own unique way. Your life's storms may be different, and your sunshine and rainbows may come in various ways, but nonetheless, you are all worthy of genuine love.

This book is the acknowledgment of a woman who exemplifies resilience in love and life, my mother. Her heart and generosity at times seem humanly impossible. She gives at the cost of her own self, and so she earned the nickname "Mother Teresa." To know her is to know the true meaning of love, charity, and forgiveness. These are qualities that most of us mere mortals only aspire to but never truly master. Yet, this woman perseveres in her journey of wanting to love and be loved.

My mother is the woman who first taught me by her example what it means to love a man, even when he stops caring for or loving you. Also, I dedicate this book to my sisters (biological and adopted), sister-aunts, and all the other amazing women in my life, who have guided and protected me on my journey of love and relationships. These women are true survivors who know how to stand through any storm that love may bring.

CHAPTER ONE

Faith

The Storm that Broke Her

As she stood in front of the stove stirring the pot of beans, she suddenly felt a thump to the left side of her head. Leo had angrily punched her again shouting, "Woman you belong to me." This all too familiar scene played out once more as if from a movie scene, rather than her life. Josie sat quietly in the corner of the little kitchen on Rose Avenue. Her heart racing as she witnessed, once again, her father's countless acts of rage.

She could feel the blood rush to her face and her ears burned as she herself burned with anger. She wished she could strike back at this cruel being who seemed to be devoid of any human feelings. His eyes appeared to glow like shiny embers of light. They looked as if they could be glaring from the face of some vile serpent. A snake ready to attack its feeble, innocent prey. Faith cowered in fear as her shoulders hunched inwardly, and she quickly lifted her hands to her face in preparation for whatever next blow might be coming her way. Josie, her daughter, watched once more as the all too familiar horrific scene played out before her eyes. The thoughts started to roar in Josie's head as the storm engulfed her sanity once more. Her mother had seemed to have gotten used to this type of abusive treatment. But Josie had not and never would. After this attack, she would be left once again to recover from its damage. Some storms come with warnings, but it was shown to Josie that the storms of love would always come suddenly and with vengeance, destroying everything of beauty associated with love. Josie blinked back the warm liquid of her salty tears, as her throat tightened and she swallowed, bracing herself to stand and face the storm. Not her own; her mother's. But it is as if she could feel her mother's hurt and pain. Her thoughts continued to rage on and she wondered, "Why doesn't she just do something? How could she just stand in stillness enduring pain, all in the name of love?" This kind of love was all Josie knew or had seen. But somehow, she knew that this was not the way love was supposed to play out. It was not the kind of love she aspired to find. Yet, for her mother, it was all she knew and somehow, all she was willing to settle for, despite its harshness.

Leo made his exit after his violent attack, like that of a snake. He struck his victim, then quickly slithered away as if his actions were just a normal part of his everyday existence. He took no note of the young woman in the corner of the kitchen. He had beaten Faith in front of the kids before, so Josie's presence had no effect on his behavior. It seemed that the audience never had any effect on Leo's performance. He would morph into his devilish character, as if he was oblivious to his surroundings and had no control over what he was becoming. He executed his theatrics and then exited the scene, ignoring the storm he had just created. He left both women in the midst of the storm to either stand and recover, or simply fall to its devastation.

As Faith's body trembled with fear, she cried as if the tears would simply wash away the pain. This reaction was all too familiar to Josie, who simply walked over to her mother and threw her arms around her repeating, as always, "It's going to be okay Ma." Faith remained silent for a moment, then abruptly left the kitchen, storming after Leo into the living room. Leo had already settled down in the floral, blue, polyester sofa, watching his usual CNN news as if he had not interacted with anyone or was unaware

2

of the storm he had just brewed up. Faith sopped the tears away with the sleeves of her blouse and she stood firmly in front of Leo. Her sleeved figure, which had drastically changed over the last few months, not from dieting but rather from stress, was now stronger than ever. She had found her voice in this moment, and she bravely peered into Leo's now calm eyes and spoke with conviction. "You are nothing but a coward; you will hit me, a woman, but you can't even stand up to a man. I'm done with you," she growled at him through the tears. Josie was now at the stove, stirring the pots, but she could clearly hear every single word her mother uttered. The words which would change the course of not only Faith's life that day, but also that of her four daughters. This time, she had meant her threat of leaving her abusive marriage. She was ready to start a new life.

Josie could recall countless times when her mother had threatened to leave her abusive marriage, but somehow, today, her conviction seemed stronger than ever. Her voice now husky from crying, continued with shouts of, "I want a divorce, you will never put your hands on me again, and I am not going back with you this time." If these words were said in Belize, Leo may have just sheepishly grinned at Faith like he usually does, totally disregarding her threats. But, after his last trip to the United States, which ended in the New York police escorting him away, he knew better this time. Leo's calm was now changing with Faith's threats and his eyes started to morph into the glowing rage he would always muster right before he brewed up a storm. But, as if by some divine force, the rage quickly subsided and he stood up from the sofa, shouting back, "Woman, I don't need you." It was as if he came back to reality from some altered universe and realized where he was and how badly this scene could play out. The realization that Faith could once more call the police to intervene gave Leo a new approach to dealing with Faith's threats. He hastily gathered his few belongings into the small carry-on bag, his only possession this trip, and stormed out of the apartment. He slammed the door with such force that Josie could tell he was gone even from the distance of the kitchen, and she knew that the storm had passed. There was now a quietness in the air, as if a cleansing had occurred. Only the bubbling of the pot of red beans could now be heard in the kitchen. There was an eerie quiet; a calmness that had now engulfed the entire apartment. This was the familiar after-storm effect. Whenever Leo had gone off in a rage or was engaged in one of his abusive episodes, he would take his leave right after, as if to flee before he could witness the damage. Today was no different.

Faith walked back into the kitchen, and back to the stove to finish dinner as she knew her daughters, grandkids and all the other adopted "family members" would be over soon. They would sit and gather in the little kitchen and dining area to enjoy the usual delicious Belizean meal she prepared daily for her family. As she went on with the seemingly choreographed cooking, she briefed Josie on her well-thought-out plans for leaving Leo. Josie was skeptical, but somehow hopeful that her mother would finally realize her worth and move on to a "better life," even if it meant they had to struggle financially. In fact, Leo's financial contribution to the family's living expenses was very limited. Josie knew her mother was a hard-working woman and somehow, she was capable of taking care of herself and her kids. Josie would often say to Faith, "Ma just leave him, we don't need him, we don't mind if we have to go live under a coconut tree with you, because that would be better than this life." Faith, of course, would always agree with her kids and would assure them that things would change. But, over the years, after twenty-eight years of marriage, it seemed to the children that they were never going to see their mother happy or with someone who was deserving of her.

For many years, Faith had tried to leave. It seemed like her entire marriage was filled with scheming one escape plan after the next. Every time she had come up with her exit plan, Leo would get wind of it and would somehow manage to convince her that things would get better, and he would change. He would vow to become the husband she had always wanted and deserved. Leo could be quite the charming man when he wanted his way, and Faith would fall for his winning charm over and over again. There was a time in the early part of the marriage when Leo had one of his affairs and was not only physically, but also verbally abusive to Faith. Somehow, the presence of another woman in their marriage would trigger Leo's violence towards Faith. It was as if he had to show her that he did not want her, and that he had "something or someone better." This time it seemed that she had enough of the abusive treatment and she was prepared to leave at any cost. The family of eight was currently residing in a small wooden house on the outskirts of the town of Sea Grape, in the southernmost area in the country of Belize. Faith was working long, endless nights with her seamstress work to provide for their current six children. Leo's small liquor shop was not doing well and whatever income he generated had to provide for his social habits, so that meant that Faith and the kids needs would often be neglected. This evening, Leo had just finished eating his dinner when Faith decided to bring up the rumors she had heard of his current affair from the ladies in town. After all, in this small town, everyone knew each other's business and the local gossip was plentiful. This particular evening, she timidly asked, "So what time will you be home tonight?" Leo mumbled his usual response of not knowing and questioning why Faith was "all of a sudden" concerned about his whereabouts. Faith could feel her heart race at his callous answer and her palms felt like sticky, moist rubber as she recalled all of the recent town gossip. All the women in town would be willing to share the details of the goings-on of Leo and his mistress. And like in most small towns, the facts could sometimes become embellished, and the story would be contoured to fit whatever the cackling women would want to convey to Faith.

Leo's anger had suddenly started to bubble forth as Faith continued with her accusations. His green eyes glared like those of a predator waiting to pounce on its prey. He shouted obscenities at Faith, and as she raised her voice and angrily responded, he jumped up from the table and struck her across the face with a painful slap that jolted her to the side. Faith felt a burning sensation across her left cheek, and she quickly shielded her face with her right arm in anticipation of a second blow. The salty tears burned her eyes as the painful blow signaled that she must surrender at this point and only her quiet whimpers could be heard as Leo angrily stormed out. His old, black, Ford pickup roared down the dusty path, and only then could Faith sit and let out her cry. Her body was shaking in agony more so from the sharp, bitter words Leo had uttered than from the striking blow. He had said that he no longer loved her, he had criticized the way she looked and made her feel so small and inadequate despite all she was doing for him as his wife and the mother of their children. His angry words played again in her ears as if from a bad movie track. "You are nothing to me woman! I am tired of all this bullshit." His ranting and raving would usually go on with a barrage of curse words and loud screaming. However, tonight Leo seemed to have a pending engagement and he was a little quicker with his blow and his abusive speech was cut short by his need to exit quickly. Despite the expedited attack, the damage was done and was not any less hurtful to Faith. In her mind, Faith resolved once more to leave a man who obviously had no love for her and who despite all she did for him and his children, would never give her the respect and appreciation that she rightly deserved. In the end, a mother's love is what motivated her to take care of her children, but a man's appreciation is usually what spurred her to take care of her man. For Faith, this lack of admiration or gratitude from Leo had caused her to feel differently; she knew her feelings for him were definitely changing. She felt she could no longer take the pain, hurt, and degradation. It was as if she was desperate to run, to hide, to leave this storm that was pummeling her heart and soul. She thought of the kids' well-being for a moment, but then her will to go on was stifled.

She felt the walls of abuse had surrounded her with such a torrential down-pour that she had to escape, or at least, seek refuge.

Her escapes were never well-thought-out plans since the urge would only occur after the abuse. The in-between time of "making up" was always hopeful. Leo would always come back after one of his attacks and make amends with Faith. He frequently would have an excuse as to why he lashed out at his wife. The blame was always something "Faith did" to make him angry. But, tonight, like countless other nights, was no different. Faith had enough at the moment and could only think of a way to end this nightmarish part of her life, and perhaps, escape was the only solution.

Faith ran out into the night after the children had gone off to sleep. She had nowhere to go but to the bushes that surrounded their house. She was not thinking clearly, and she didn't have a plan. She just knew she could not breathe freely in that home that had become her prison. She needed to escape. In the dark coat of the night, she ran to a nearby coconut tree, where she stopped to catch her breath. The crickets could be heard chirping, the gentle breeze of the night swayed through the trees and the rustling of leaves added to the eerie vibe of the night. It was as if she was suddenly transported to another place. The night's darkness was thick; the blackness made it impossible for one to even see the space for the next step. There was a chill of coolness that suddenly engulfed her body, even though she could feel the warmth on her forehead as droplets of perspiration moistened her skin. For a moment, Faith became afraid. She thought of how stupid it was of her to run out into the unknown of the forest, leaving her innocent children sleeping oblivious to what was occurring. But her fear quickly waned as her mind raced back to all the times, she had attempted to leave Leo, only to go back into the same storms of love that had beat her down. The torrential rain of pain, of hurt, of love lost and of a realization of the loss of hope.

Sleep and exhaustion had eventually set in for Faith and she could feel her swollen eyes drooping. She had tried to find a comfortable spot under the coconut tree, but the dry, brittle branches on the ground poked into her back and she could not find comfort or solace. The night was getting creepier as strange noises could be heard in the distance. Faith knew of all the wild animals that lurked in the forest. The forest of Sea Grape was notorious for the jaguars who were vicious predators or even a venomous "Tommy Goffe" snake. She knew that she would be easy prey with no defense. Perhaps she could go back and face Leo's wrath later. He had obviously gotten his discontent out, so he would likely return with a different attitude. Or Faith could simply curl up in her corner of the queen size bed and fake sleep as she had done on countless other nights. After all, the baby would be waking up soon and all the older kids would be sleeping soundly, unable to hear the cries of her little, frail, baby girl. It is in the moments of greatest challenges that a mother will sacrifice everything for her children. Faith was no different. She could not allow her children to be neglected or to suffer because of the turmoil of her marriage. She had to go back and face what the rains of Leo's new affair would bring. She reasoned that she would still leave in the future, but only with a well-thought-out plan. So, through the darkness of the night she hastily made her way back home.

CHAPTER TWO

Faith

The Weather Is Unpredictable

To understand your current place in life, you sometimes must go back and revisit your past. Especially when it comes to matters of the heart. To know why our "love storms" are created, we must first understand what triggers them. Love will first come with beautiful sunshiny days. Like the dawn of a new day, there is always a bright start that beckons you to embrace it with great enthusiasm. You might say it's the weather that allows a woman to glow and bask in the "rays of love." Supposedly, that is why a person is said to glow or beam when they are in love. It is only at the end of a love story that the torrential rains will wash away that glow. For those who grow in love, the glow will usually never fade; in fact, it becomes more prominent with time. Love nurtures the glow that will continue to radiate if love is able to mature. But the pain of unrequited love can have the opposite effect on someone. Loss of love will usually leave a darkness and sadness that is evident when a heart is broken. For many women, even when that glow is not nurtured, they will hope still, and continue to hope for sunshine. A woman always wants to stay with the man she loves, even when he hurts her. Perhaps, it is the feminine trait of being a nurturer that keeps a woman trying to win in love. So, she might weather through the drizzle and believe that the sun will soon shine again.

Faith loved Leo; she had started her life with him as a teen, believing in the longevity of that love. Their life wasn't always bad, in fact, there were times when she was hopeful. The beginning had started with sunshine. In fact, she had dreamt of a life where they would have a family and live as an old married couple. After all, Leo was one of the most eligible bachelors in the small town of Sea Grape. Leo came from what one would consider a well-to-do family in this little isolated town by the sea. Sea Grape was a place where everything was unique as compared with the rest of the world. Love was kind of different here as well. Women were expected to be house-wives and to obey their husbands at whatever cost. Love was not about romance but more about the practical notion of raising a family and to carrying on the next generation with stability. Her grandmother had said it countless times, "You are lucky to have a man like that from such a good family." But luck was never on Faith's side in her tumultuous marriage.

Initially, Faith's focus was on getting an education and establishing a career for herself. She was always told that she was a smart girl. In fact, she excelled in math, which often brought her much praise from her teach-ers. She was admired not only for her academic skills but was also given unwanted physical attention by some of her male teachers. Faith was deter-mined to get her high school education and dreamt of one day becoming a teacher. Nonetheless, life had other plans for her. She never finished high school and become one of the many high school drop-outs in her small town. It was as if women in this town were seldom successful as career-women. Many of the women would never start a secondary education, and becoming a mother and housewife was, eventually, their future. Faith's grandmother wanted better for her granddaughter, and she supported her in wanting to go to high school and have a career. The family had made sacrifices for this goal. Faith was bright and ambitious and there was much hope in her. She was supposed to defy the odds.

But life has a way of changing course when we least expect it. One evening, walking home with her usual group of friends from high school, Faith's destiny was changed in an instant by her meeting the infamous Leo. That meeting would forever alter the course of her life and change the woman she was to become. Perhaps, if Faith had insight into the future, during this meeting she would have kept walking, ignoring the glance from Leo, as she usually did when boys would give her attention. But one look into the face of this tall, skinny, young man and she was immediately mesmerized. Leo had an unusually handsome face, which stood out in this little town. He was not only six foot one, towering over most men, but his green eyes would dazzle most people since they were a very unique genetic trait among the inhabitants of Sea Grape. He had the face of a movie star and later in his life, he was frequently mistaken for the late Anthony Bourdain. The girls in her class had spoken often of the eligible bachelors in town and since they were all at the bloom of womanhood, finding a mate was a foremost quest. Of course, Leo was at the top of the list for most of these eager young women. That memorable evening came to mind often for Faith. She often thought of what she could have done differently had she kept her determination firm to not get involved with anyone until she was finished with high school. However, this day had changed everything. The girls were dressed as usual in their white high school uniforms and Faith's black hair was neatly pulled back in a ponytail as she would often wear it. This allowed for her high cheekbones and her beautiful face to be even more prominent. She had a dark, dewy complexion and her sultry eyes were captivating. Faith was definitely a beauty, but somehow, she never believed it. But this particular evening as Leo approaches the group of girls, Faith had hope that she was attractive enough to draw his attention. She had seen Leo around town countless times, but always from a distance. She had heard her girlfriends rave over his handsomeness, but she felt that she was not easily swayed by physical appearance. Beverly, the loudest of the girls, and the most brazen, shouted at Leo as she strutted forward. "Hello, Bev! Where are you beautiful ladies headed to?" Leo answered as he flashed his winning smile. Beverly had a boyfriend but would never miss an opportunity to flirt with any handsome man. Also, she wanted to brag to her friends that she knew the charming Leo. "Why don't you introduce me to your beautiful friend here?" he continued as he gestured toward, the now blushing, Faith. Leo and Faith clearly knew each other, since in the small town of Sea Grape, everyone knew each other in some way or had mutual friends or acquaintances. "I know him," Faith shyly responded to Beverly. She smiled timidly at Leo and said, "Well, I guess we haven't really spoken to each other personally, so it's nice then to officially meet you." Leo had wasted no time in making his intentions known. "But I would like to know you much better." He responded slyly with the usual gleam in his piercing green eyes. "How about I walk you home from school tomorrow?" Faith was flattered, she was looking around at the group as if needing reassurance from her friends that this was acceptable to do. Beverly, the usual spokesperson for the group, quickly confirmed to Leo that, indeed, Faith would be glad to have his company. Faith could feel her heart race; her palms had suddenly become moist and sticky from perspiration. She had never been in love, in fact, she was at a point in her life where men were not a focus. But here was one of the most charming guys in town giving her attention. She was exhilarated, but she had said "no," fearing retaliation from her grandmother. However, her initial hesitation had not deterred Leo. Clearly, he knew he could get almost any woman he wanted in this town, so when the smart, beautiful Faith first shunned his advances, he persisted in his pursuit of her. It was only a matter of time before Faith had fallen completely under his spell. This was the start of a new chapter in her life. Faith eventually had to confess to her grandmother about her secret love affair with Leo. Of course, her grandma not only approved, to Faith's amazement, but was excited that she had gotten the attention of one of the most eligible bachelors. After all, she was getting old and had worried about what would become of Faith when she was gone. And so, with her grandmother's consent, the courtship had begun.

In the cool evenings on the small, dimly lit front porch, Leo would often sit with Faith and court her in hopes of one day making her his wife. He had a way with words and somehow always made her feel as if she might be missing a "prize" if she continued to shun his prospect of marriage. On one particular evening, after Grandmother Jemma had gone to bed, Faith found herself in the thick mist of Leo's irresistible charm. This night he had clearly put a lot of attention into looking his best. His curly brown hair shone in the glowing beams of the moonlight. His face had a particular glow and Faith couldn't tell if it was the Brylcream (a local beauty cream) or just his happiness that was causing this aura. His luminous eyes were like emeralds and Faith had a hard time looking into his face without dispelling the secrets of her heart, or the hot rhapsody that had engulfed her entire body. But even with her shy glances and pretense of disinterest, Leo knew for sure he had gotten Faith under his spell, and she would now be his for the taking. Their passion had progressed from the awkward peck on the lips to a full-on "make-out" session on this given night. Leo had lunged over to sit beside Faith on the creaky wooden bench, he tightly embraced her and whispered all the promises that Faith had longed for and that was the beginning of their romance.

Grandma Jemma was only too glad to welcome Leo into her home. She would quickly usher him in, with much delight in his courtship visits. The little wooden house on stilts was small, but always immaculately clean, with some small touches like that of some aristocratic British family. Ironing sheets, pillows cases and every piece of linen was usually a nuisance to Faith. However, during these courtship visits, Faith was pleased by the high-end touches throughout their little cottage, as it made her feel less embarrassed about Leo's presence in their space. In stark contrast, Leo lived about half a mile away on Main Street in one of the grandest houses in Sea Grape. His father being a sugar mill manager and then the political area representative, ensured that his family was well provided for materially. Leo never made Faith feel less than, despite his mother's objections to courting a dark-skinned, creole girl. He thought she was beautiful and a worthy partner. Perhaps this was the reason Faith was more drawn to him despite the flaws she was now beginning to see in his character. Their relationship had gotten serious. However, this fact had changed nothing for Leo in his responsibilities in life. He carried on with his single bachelor lifestyle. Coming from some means meant Leo could live life on his own terms. Early on, he told his father he would not go to high school and chose instead to work on the family farm. In a few months of dating, life had changed for the couple, and they eventually married.

As a young husband, Leo would soon learn that Dad could not take care of him anymore and he would have to go out and work to support his wife and kids. Life with Leo was not only an emotional struggle, but it was also a physical and financial struggle for Faith. During her second year of high school, she became pregnant with her and Leo's first child. Her grandmother had demanded that they get married, as she would not be embarrassed by her granddaughter's pregnancy out of wedlock. "You can't raise a bastard child," her grandmother had insisted. Grandma Jemma was a woman of "class and good breeding," or at least that's how she thought of herself. The thought of the town gossiping about her granddaughter's pregnancy was the kind of shame she would not stand for in her family. She had always prided herself on her moral and social standing in the town of Sea Grape, so she would not let Faith tarnish that image in any way. But for Faith and Leo, marriage meant their lives would never be the same. Faith was only three months pregnant when Leo had proposed. Grandma Jemma had made it clear to Leo what her expectations of him were in moving forward with her granddaughter. One evening during his evening visits, Grandma Jemma stood in the doorway of the small dimly lit house, awaiting the suitor. Her towering six-foot silhouette, dressed in her crisp starch white cotton dress was quite an intimidating presence, and Leo recognized immediately that something was not right. He had discussed with Faith that they would not tell Grandma Jemma of the pregnancy until they had a definite plan, and he being the man, he wanted to gently break the horrid news. Unfortunately, Faith's first trimester was very eventful as she had morning sickness in the worst possible way. She would wake up in the mornings retching the bilious contents of her stomach with such noise and urgency that it would awaken the household. "Girl, what's wrong with you?" Her grandmother had accusingly asked one morning. Grandma Jemma had already figured out that Faith was pregnant early on, she was just waiting for the imminent confession. Faith was left with no choice but to sadly reveal her frightening secret. She feared Leo's intentions, but even more so she was dreading her grandmother's reaction. Luckily Grandma Jemma took the news much better than expected. "I knew that boy was up to no good, but I hope he realizes that he will have to marry you right away and make this thing right. At least he is decent enough and I'm getting old, so you need a husband," she had gone on and on scolding Faith.

As a high school dropout, Leo could not afford to give Faith a real wedding. In fact, he had to borrow money from his father to pay for the marriage certificate and the required elements. Faith's grandmother was too frail to attend the simple church service. In Leo's family, there was staunch disapproval of marrying a girl like Faith, especially from Leo's mother. So, on a warm, quiet afternoon, the young couple tied the knot with only two guests in attendance. The little Catholic church near the seaside was unusually solemn that evening; it was as if a funeral was happening rather than a joyous wedding. This was not the wedding Faith had dreamt of, but she thought, at least she was getting married and making her grand-mother's wishes come true. Leo's best friend had shown up as his best man, but Faith had stood alone, in her mini white dress, solemnly agreeing to a lifetime with a stranger. A young man she had come to love deeply despite the red flags that were now evident in their relationship.

The newlywed couple struggled to survive. A few months after their first daughter, Destiny, was born, Faith suffered a miscarriage and quickly became pregnant with her second child. The children just came consecutively and soon after the birth of their third child, Josie, Faith began working long hours. Life was hard, and she had not gotten the support from her husband that she expected. She had to feed her kids as Leo was now drowning his struggles with family life in the intoxicating effects of the white rum sold at the local rum shops. Faith could no longer rely on Leo as his drinking got worse. She did not have a high school education and so her options for earning a living were limited. After being forced to sew clothes for her children from any scraps of fabric she could find, her skill as a seamstress soon soared. She was charging to make clothes, especially uniforms for the local town kids, and word of her excellent workmanship soon got around town. "Ms. Faith sews really good, and she charges cheap," the women of the town would eagerly spread word of her talent. Faith had quickly become known as "one of the best seamstresses in town," and she would get so much work, that she would have to stay up late into the night to keep up with her growing business. Never in her wildest dreams did she imagine she would become a seamstress. But life has a way of sometimes leading us to our destiny in strange ways. In addition to her seamstress work, her time was further strained by her growing brood of children.

Their third child, Josie, was only a year old when Faith became pregnant with her fourth child. This ever-growing family trend was not a strange phenomenon in Sea Grape, as most of the families had many children. There was no way for women in the town to get any kind of medical obstetric or gynecological care, except for delivery of their babies or basic prenatal visits. Birth control was not a viable option. The small-town hospital had services for everything from a trauma victim to delivery of an infant. There was one doctor in town, who took care of the entire town's population. Preventative care was never discussed or available. So, pregnancies were often unplanned and unwanted. In fact, quite a few deliveries would happen at home under the care of one of the two local midwives. Childbearing was an integral part of a woman's life. One would simply conceive and have many children as the Catholic faith was prevalent in the town and would not allow for abortions. Women were seen as child bearers, and to do or think otherwise was not the popular view. Faith was no different. In fact, she never even paid much attention to her menstrual cycles as she would often still be breastfeeding her infant when she would become pregnant with her next child. That was her life, and she simply accepted it as all of the women in that little, rural town did. Besides, continuing to produce the next generation, women were also often the main caregivers of that generation. Men were only there to provide materially as breadwinners and often, that role would default to the women as well in this town, as in the case of Faith. You would be considered lucky if your man provided fully for you financially. In fact, most women who had husbands who worked full time would still have to do some kind of work to help supplement the family's income. Many women would make baked goods or sell food items. Some would have to resort to gardening or rather, have a "plantation," a small plot of land that was used to grow food to help sustain many of the large families.

Josie recalled many nights when they would all doze off around the little old Singer machine at her mother's feet. The scraps of material would quickly gather around the perimeter of the machine, forming a somewhat soft spot to lay. Every piece of fabric was different in shape, color, and design. But besides being bedding, the children also found inspiration for crafting. This was particularly the case with her third child, Josie. As if an apprentice, she would watch and learn as her mother worked. Josie would pick up every scrap and scrutinize each piece as she imagined all the possibilities she could create. At her mother's foot is where Josie first tapped into her own creative side and soon learned that she not only had a little of her mother's knack for crafting, but for cooking as well. She would mimic and bother her mother from time to time as to how she could cut her doll's dress or how to stitch together the pieces. These skills had later served her well in her adult life.

But, as the children grew up and their needs got more expensive; life became difficult. Faith would spend many long nights at her little old Singer machine, not only sewing for her customers, but also sewing her children's clothing as well. Her money was limited, and she knew she had to stretch it as far as she could. So, that meant the kids would often wear hand-me-downs and getting store-bought clothing, or any other item was a luxury not often afforded. Most of the children in the small town faced similar economic hardships, so Faith's children never felt out of place or deprived. In fact, compared to most, they were privileged somehow to just have all their basic needs adequately met. "You guys have it good," the children would often hear from their friends and neighbors. They knew that having enough food and never going hungry was not the case for other children in the town. Also, watching their peers in torn, tattered clothes and some running around barefooted, drove home the knowledge of their somewhat privileged life in this small town.

Another of the children's benefits of having an industrious mother was her ability to tell the most captivating stories. Books were a luxury and so Faith would often entertain the children with her stories. The clanking of the old metal machine did not hinder the family's favorite past-time of storytelling. Faith would tell the kids stories of local fables and myths. Among the children's favorite was the tales of the gullible "Tiger and the Cunning Bra Anansi." The storytelling would often end with all the kids curled up at the foot of her machine, dozing off to slumber. As Faith would feel the tiredness of her long day weigh in, she would not have the strength to carry each child to bed. So, like everything else in their family routine, the older ones would have to help with their younger siblings. She would awaken each one ever so gently to help with the task of moving their younger siblings to bed. Josie had especially hated this task as she herself would be tired and would begrudgingly drag her younger sister, Gia, into the tiny bed they shared. Life was hard, but the family seemed to be happy despite alcoholism and poverty. Faith's joy was her children. She did her best to provide for them and many nights would forego her own share of meat at dinner to ensure that the children all ate. In fact, the children would always notice their mother's plate with the bones or bony parts of the meat, somehow, they had over the years taken a liking to bones, imitating their mother's share and would often argue over who would get the bones. This phenomenon was especially the case with her daughters. Faith had found this strange, but somehow, she would recall her grandmother's words of "children learn what they live," and in some strange way, it made sense. At other times it meant that the large family would have to stretch the little food to ensure that everyone ate. For example, the eggs would miraculously multiply by adding baking powder and so everyone could get a decent share of egg. It wasn't until years later that the children would laugh at this obscure cooking practice as food became more commonplace. Sadly, it was not particular to just their family, in fact, it was their adopted brother who introduced the practice that he had grown up with in his own deprived family.

Survival in this little town was a struggle for most of its inhabitants. Even though Faith and Leo were considered middle class, it meant that most people were living well below their financial class. But life in Sea Grape town was a continued battle for this couple despite their standing in the society at large. Yet, this did not stop Faith from stretching the little she had, to give a meal to most of the kid's friends who would hang around for countless hours. Many of the boys were sort of adopted into the large family. In fact, one teenager ended up moving in with the family and eventually became a member of the large brood of children. Daniel was a friend of the oldest brother but somehow, he eventually became friend to all the kids. He was very good with caring for the younger children and would often carry the baby around on his hips or pull her in his wooden cart truck that he had built himself. The baby could often be heard squealing in delight as she was entertained by this now-adopted older brother. This gawky, industrious teenager was just the Godsend Faith needed. He was not only very helpful with the kids but would also help with the chores around the house. It was never really clear when he was accepted into the family, he somehow seemed like he just always belonged with them. Years later, his biological mother who had lived in the United States, sent for him to have a better life, But by then other adoptive kids had already joined the growing gang.

After ten years of marriage, Leo and Faith now had eight children, and providing for such a large family was a daunting task. Nevertheless, the economic hardships of life in the little town never discouraged the people. Many women would grow most of the family food, and this was the only way to keep starvation at bay. Life was not about romance or love for many of these women; it was simply about survival; feeding their children and providing for their basic needs. Putting food on the table was the focus of their day. A woman in these times would simply suffocate her dreams of living in love or being showered with love. Life was merely about survival. Relationships were about satisfying physical needs mostly, and so these women were emotionally starving.

It appears these females were never allowed to be women. Clothing, jewelry, and other female items were often a luxury few women got to indulge in. A woman was often seen with her head covered or braided so as not to hinder her work, her skin would be burned and weathered from the harsh rays of the sun, her feet often in flip flops or rubber boots. Dressing and grooming were not a priority. Faith would spend most of her days dressed in the simple cotton dresses she had sewed herself and her hair always plainly braided. Femininity was rarely seen, except on special occasions when the women would adorn themselves with colorful clothes and jewelry, most of which were handmade. As for the few aristocratic women of the town whose husbands provided for them financially, they somehow were able to live a more privilege lifestyle. These were the few shop owners or other merchants who were considered the elites of the town. These families were able to afford more for their children as well. Often, the wives of these merchants would not work and would be "kept housewives." Most women in Sea Grape would have to work hard and had innovated many ways to provide for the basic needs of their families. It often meant not only working outside of the home, but also working within the home as a housewife as well. Life was hard in this little town. Yet, a woman will always do whatever it takes to make sure her children are provided for materially. This was the case for Faith. As a mother, she often neglected herself and focused on taking care of her children. Eventually, this took a toll on not only her well-being, but it also was perhaps one of the main reasons for her marriage breakdown. She never felt feminine. She sometimes felt like a robot merely performing the functions of her daily life. Leo was merely a partner in some respects, but largely she was on her own performing her many duties. His companionship was very limited and their couple time was limited to the few minutes before sleeping. The love between them was strained and often, Faith would wonder if he had even loved her still after the first few years. Love was hard to find for most women in this town. Love was more about storms than sunshine.

CHAPTER THREE

Faith

The Storm of Divorce and New Love

Divorce had not come as a surprise solution to Faith. Nonetheless, a divorce can sometimes hit like lightning despite the expectation of it. The hard years were behind her, at least in most aspects of her life. Faith had to learn early on to survive and take care of her eight children. This meant that she had to become innovative. She had ventured into many businesses, starting with her sewing. However, as clothes were not a necessity, but food was; she eventually opened a small grocery store to sustain her family. Over the years of doing business, her future was looking better financially as her marriage deteriorated. Faith had eventually become a store owner of one of the main grocery stores in town and her business was successful. Yet her marriage continued to fail and the end of her life with Leo was eminent. Generally, women in Sea Grape were expected to stay with their men even if they cheated or abused them. This was a town where traditions were upheld, and the Catholic faith had a strong following. But for Faith, divorce made sense. Yet, its effects can still be devasting, even when one has resolved to leave as it is the best solution. There seemed to be an attachment of familiarity that keep women with men who are of no value to them. Starting over with someone new, or even alone is never easy. It is as if you must relearn the familiar things of your life and day-to-day routine. The new smell of that person, the little annoying quirks that you have learned to ignore. The routine of your day-to-day life that has almost become like a dance that you have mastered. Yes, starting over is uncomfortable, it is challenging. But for the brave ones who survive it, they can flourish in whatever new situation they find themselves in. The new will somehow become familiar again and it's as if a new dance is learned. It can be a positive life altering event. It changes the way a woman sees herself and sometimes she goes through a major makeover in every sense, including her appearance. It is often said that a woman will blossom when she feels beautiful. Like a flower, her beauty will mesmerize others, and it is as if she can continue to bloom anew just like a withering flower dies and re-blooms again. Faith now felt beautiful as she entered this new phase of her life. It seemed as if the divorce was some kind of watering that she needed to blossom into the confident, stylish woman that was now strutting around the apartment on Rose Avenue in Chicago. Life had taken her to a new place, a new country, and she was starting over with a new life in America. Chicago was the city that her eldest daughter, Destiny, was now living in with her first husband, who was a native of the area. Faith's life was now fertilized by her moving to a new country and starting over without Leo. She had migrated to America to get away from him; still, she had not officially filed for divorce right away. But this was her way of providing financially for her children and gaining her emotional independence. That last blow he had struck her in the little kitchen on Rose Avenue had changed everything. In time, the divorce was filed and finalized, and life was moving on in a whole new direction. Over the last few months, after her divorce, she started to metamorphize into the beauty she had kept hidden for so many years during her marriage. Always the plain jane, Faith never gave much thought to her physical appearance. Her time was generally consumed by attending to her demanding husband's needs and that of her eight children. But now that she was freed from the confines of her marriage, she took a renewed interest in her looks. Faith would now roll her hair in curls; gone were the usual cornrow braids or single ponytail. Her thick black hair was now considered stylish. Now she took pride in presenting her best face to the world. Makeup now became a part of her daily routine as well. Her beautiful dark, soulful eyes would now be lined with various bright colors to match her outfits. Essentially, she was now "feeling herself" as her daughters would joke to her. There was now a commanding presence in her face, as she would color her lips often with her favorite color, red. Red was always her favorite color, but in the past one would never have guessed, since it was never present in her old grooming. It was as if she had hidden who she was in the dark, drab clothing that was part of her wardrobe during her marriage. Faith was a curvy, black woman, but she never wore anything clingy, so one would never see the womanly curves she had kept hidden under the plain cotton dresses she wore during her marriage. In fact, Leo was a very jealous man, so she was sure to not draw any undue male attention to herself, as this would result in a heated fight with Leo. But, as she changed her marital status, she also did the same to her external appearance. It was like a butterfly leaving its cocoon. This transformation was not only evident to her family, but she also drew the attention of the opposite sex, which felt good to Faith; for once she was beginning to feel womanly. Something Faith had long forgotten during her gruesome years as a wife and mother. Beauty and attraction were new again and it allowed her to once more dream of the love and romance she had always wanted in her life. One of her many suitors had gotten her attention and had convinced her to go on a date. Her life had now included three of her daughters also moving to America and that meant she also now had their support in her new pursuit of romance. She was determined to not only make life different for herself, but also for her children. The girls had cheered on this new woman, this new phase of her life which included dating and her blossoming into a butterfly.

The dating arena was a new thing for both mother and daughters, but in America, this was a commonplace practice and was part of establishing relationships. On one particular date, her daughters had looked on in awe as their mother stood in front of the mirror adjusting a strand of black curl from her now made-up face. Josie smiled as she gazed at her mother thinking how beautiful she looked in her floral pink dress and pouty red lips. It was strange that she had never thought of her mother's beauty until now. It was as if it was hidden on purpose so as not to attract any attention and to focus on the daily grind of life. But this was different; this was a new phase for the butterfly woman that was now flaunting her beauty. Faith was about to embark on her first real date. Leo had been the only man in her life, and they had never really gone out on dates. His courtship was short and always under the watchful eyes or ears of Grandma Jemma. People in the town of Sea Grape had never really dated in those days. Most marriages were arranged, or courtship was merely going from initial physical attraction to physical manifestation of that chemistry and onto shacking up. But today, she was all smiles, and she giggled as she described meeting this handsome Mexican, Alejandro.

Her phone rang and she sweetly answered, as her date was now waiting outside the apartment and summoning her presence. Like a giddy teenager, Faith was ecstatic about this date. Perhaps, it was because she not only felt valued by this man, but she was also feeling what it was like to be admired and loved. Faith grabbed her pink purse to match the rest of her carefully thought-out outfit. Of course, all her girls had given their input, because to them, this date was the important start of a new life for their mother. The women all rushed to the window to get a glimpse of the handsome man that stole their mother's heart. Alejandro stood with a big grin on the sidewalk. His black curly hair was shiny, and well groomed, and of course, the green suit with matching black shoes and shirt meant that he also had put a lot of effort preparing for this date. The girls tried to hold back their excitement and giddy laughing so as not to bring any attention to their sneaking glances. They could not help the joy they felt as they were seeing love in their mother's eyes. Most children desire to see their parents happy, and this time it was no different. Love had never shown up much in their parent's marriage. Perhaps it was there, but it was never evident. Somehow the children had deciphered that their mother did love their father; why else would a woman put up with all that abuse? There were times of small stolen acts of affection, but they were few and far in between. A quick tap on the buttocks or a small peck on the cheek was all that Leo ever expressed publicly. Also, the language of love was hardly ever spoken in their childhood, as their father would often address their mother usually with harsh words, discontentment or blaming of some sort. If love is not shown or experienced, one can become accustomed to not having it. The girls were aware of what it was and should look like but often, it only existed in their minds, seen in movies, as a dream rather than reality. This was love seen in action, this was new to them, but this was what they had all dreamt of for their mother.

Sadly, love does not always take the journey we want. Even with the right person and the right circumstances, life sometimes gets in the way. It is as if that kind of love is only reserved for a few lucky women. This was the case for Faith and Alejandro. Despite their falling in love with each other, the relationship was short-lived. Alejandro's mother fell gravely ill, and he needed to move back to Mexico to care for her. Alejandro took care of his mother, and she was dear to him. Faith knew because of his close relationship with his mother that he was, in return, going to be good to her as well. Her grandmother had often told her that "you can tell the way a man is going to treat you by the way he treats his mother." He had begged Faith to come with him. In fact, he had even proposed marriage to Faith.

But as a mother and now grandmother, Faith could not leave her children and grandchildren. She thought that at her age she had no business following some man to a country she never dreamed of living in. Faith had visited Alejandro's family in Mexico and would often recount to her daughters how well the family had treated her. She spoke Spanish fluently, so it would not have been a difficult transition. Her time in Mexico was like a fairytale. Faith would often rave on about the beautiful flowers Alejandro would give to her, as he knew how passionate she was about flowers. She would smile as she told the girls of the romantic walks and beautiful gondola rides, she and Alejandro would take during their time together. Faith was in love with this man and her life with him was more like sunshine and rainbows; storms were now a thing of the past. They had continued a long-distance relationship even after Alejandro had moved back, but somehow love does not always make the heart grow fonder. Distance can eventually stretch a relationship into oblivion. In the end, they could not sustain the ties of their love. The distance and with time, that phase of Faith's life had fizzled out.

Over the years, she dated other men infrequently, but was never quite smitten again as she had been with Alejandro. Often, her daughter would listen with empathy as she recalled, "the best days of my life." The girls themselves had also had their share of love and loss. Their lives had all taken them on different journeys. Time had forged love in and out of their lives. Men had come and gone. Some stayed on for a season or reason, but their lives were somehow always riddled with the dooming storms of love. The daughters sought desperately the love they were never given by their father, but as if by some cruel joke of the universe, the men who came into their lives always seemed to possess some of the ugly qualities of their father. It seemed like most fatherless girls become man-less women by default. Somehow, these kinds of women can never attract the men that could give them the male love they so desperately seek. Or perhaps, even if the love they seek should manifest in their lives, they somehow could not keep it. It was as if the skills needed to keep a good man around were never learned and always lacking. Such was the case for all these women as they struggled to navigate through the storms of love.

Over the next few years, Destiny's first marriage to the husband from Chicago had ended. Josie was moving to Florida to live with her, then, boyfriend, Gia the middle daughter, had left her common-law husband and moved to the United States with her two boys, and Stacey, the youngest girl, and her son, was now in a serious relationship with her boyfriend. Faith's girls had each been through their individual storms of love. The girls' lives had been like a whirlwind of relationships as they navigated their own storms of love throughout the years. Perhaps, therefore Faith was always apprehensive about her daughters' relationships with men. She would give them endless advice about not falling into her footsteps, or about not making the same mistakes that she had made. She wanted for her girls to all be happily married; a goal she herself could not have achieved. But marriage was not the only wish Faith worked on for her daughters. She made whatever sacrifice was necessary over the years to ensure that each of her girls would achieve a good education, or at least, was given the opportunity. She had instilled the importance of making your own money, or as the creole version goes, she would often say to her children, "sleep with your own eyes."

Eventually, the sisters all ended up living together in Florida during the year of 2015. But divorce seemed eminent in their lives. It was as if Faith's legacy of failed marriage was being passed down to her daughters. It was like a family curse that these women seemed destined to encounter no matter the man or the circumstances of their individual lives. After Destiny's second marriage had failed, she had packed up whatever little belongings she kept from the ravenous Mr. Hopard and drove down to Florida with her two boys from her first marriage to start a new life. This second marriage of Destiny's had lasted less than two years from courtship to divorce. On the other hand, Gia, who had left the father of her second son, had already joined Josie and her boyfriend as roommates as she pursued her schooling, and so, she too was now in Florida. Only she had met a man who was soon to be her husband. The year 2005 was a milestone year for all the daughters. Life had brought each of them individually to the same point; all in different ways. It was shortly after Gia's move that the youngest sister, Stacey, also migrated to Florida with her young son from boyfriend Alfred, who was also in tow. Their love lives spun like a spider web, with no clear endpoint. To say the lives of these women were like a roller coaster would be an understatement. They were all seeking the same goals of being independent, successful, married women; each in their own unique way. Somehow, their paths all aligned in all being married in the same year. Also, interestingly, they all bore boys, so these sons were essentially the only men that were staple figures in their lives. These women had lives of love that involved several love storms. Each had traversed into some relationship or marriage that had somehow led to divorce or breakup.

The women had all taken different roads in their pursuit of relationships, except for in 2005, when they had all gotten married to their, then, partners. Including Faith, who had only recently started dating her Venezuelan boyfriend who was almost eighteen years her junior. This was only her second serious relationship after her divorce. Again, she was in love and ready to give her heart to another man. Only this time, he was approximately the same age as her oldest daughter, a fact that did not go over well with her daughters in the beginning. But he was a meek and humble man, and the girls knew that their mother had taken a particular liking to him. Their unlikely meeting in the apartment complex was not unusual, but for their friendship to bloom into romance was strange. He was short in stature, in fact, standing next to Faith, he seemed to have been a few inches shorter. His dark, round eyes were framed by dark brows that seemed to emit kindness. His mustache lends to the face of a chef of sorts, and in fact, that was his occupation. At first, the short, meek Venezuelan would come over and join the family for dinner, with no suspicions of any sort. But, as time went on, he would stay on for the nightly family television viewing and chatting, until he became a regular at the family gatherings. There were nights when the family would all lay out in the small confines of the living room area, like sardines in a can. This was not unusual since Faith would often cook her delicious meals to ensure that her family would gather. Some would lazily slump over on the sofa and others in chairs, while some would just lay low on the floors. But it had become apparent that Faith's new friend had become more than a friend as he would lay next to her during these family assemblies. After a time, the little Venezuelan man became fondly named "Pappi" by the grandkids and was adopted into the family as Faith's new beau.

In 2005, Faith and Pappi decided to tie the knot, and amazingly, so did her four daughters and their partners. Over the years, the women would reminisce about the five marriages in 2005. They marveled at the fact that Stacey's was done almost in secret, while Josie's seemed to have happened on a whim one day at the courthouse. Destiny's was the grandest, of course, since Mr. Hopard would not have it any other way. Destiny would recall to her sisters that she merely went with all the plans that Mr. Hopard had made, since she neither had the time or experience in wedding planning; her first marriage was at the courthouse. Years later, the family would look at the beautiful pictures of the lakeside wedding and have mixed emotions about the grand affair. Destiny had looked like a princess in her flowy halter gown as she gracefully exited the white, horse-drawn Cinderella-like carriage. The girls all had taken different routes to their destination of living happily ever after. Gia's wedding at the end of that year was also a big family affair. She had wed her husband in a beautiful family wedding near the pool of the hotel where they hosted the affair. Josie had outdone herself trying to make the wedding the memorable event she didn't have but wanted for her sister. After all, Josie's boyfriend had made certain she knew that their marriage had conditions, and he was not about a grand affair. Perhaps, it would still be lasting despite his hesitations; Josie had thought as she had to forgo everything, she had wanted for her dream wedding. Nonetheless, Gia's wedding was a happy time and as she walked down the aisle holding her new husband's hands, they both smiled and looked so happy together.

To keep up with the marriages and love lives of the sisters was like trying to navigate through a maze. There was always a lost love, or a new love who eventually would become a husband and then a failed marriage and lastly, the dreadful divorce. However, Faith's beaming glow in the year 2005, from knowing that somehow, she was married and so were all her daughters, lasted only for a little while. Her wish for them had somehow, miraculously come true in one year. Sadly, two years later, the first divorce of Josie seemed to have triggered the trend of finding and losing love. A trend that most women could identify with, but never understand. Faith and her daughters were no different than the women friends they had in Sea Grape and in America. After all, the eldest daughter, Destiny, went on to have four marriages, two after her fairytale wedding to Mr. Hopard, but then, that's another long saga of love and loss. A story which Destiny would eventually go on to tell in her own words. Common to all women everywhere are the devastating storms of love. These women were no different from any other woman around the world who was trying to find and keep love. Love and loss seemed to have been a steady event in their lives. Surviving and standing to face its elements with dignity and grace was the key. But the victims of a storm never survive without having learned some coping mechanisms. It is the lessons learned and the survival mechanisms that allow for women to stand in any of life's storms. These women had each withstood the storm's devastating effects, and each had developed her own way of weathering it.

But sometimes, to understand survival, one must understand the journey. Faith's journey was definitely a lesson in how to overcome whatever storm came your way in life. She has prevailed despite the horrors of her first marriage, and the disappointments of her second. Nonetheless, like most relationships, hers was a sunshine affair at the start. Faith's second marriage had started in bliss as most marriages do. She and Pappi had rented a small one-bedroom apartment, in close proximity to her daughters and grandkids. The family was always close to each other, and nothing changed as Pappi was easily adopted in as a new member. He was a chef by trade, and, like Faith, he loved to cook and entertain. Many of the family's dinners were lavishly done in the confines of their small apartment. Pappi would cook endlessly, and the family was always dazzled by the intricate design of his food presentations. He was a professionally trained chef who had worked on cruise ships. His pastries would often take on animal shapes which the grandkids loved, and the vegetables and fruits would never be presented in their natural forms. There would be baskets made from watermelon, and every fruit would be some unique design. Faith had not only found a love partner, but he was the best cooking partner as well. These many dinners always consisted of many courses where Pappi's culinary skills were on full display, much to everyone's delight.

Pappi was a charming addition to the family, except Faith soon began to experience another side of him that was dark and sinister. Again, her sunshiny weather seemed only short-lived, and the storms of love now loomed on the horizon. Shortly after the wedding, a friend of Pappi's would visit with Faith and told her of another side of this Venezuelan man's strange ways that were nothing like the man he appeared to be. His friend would tell of unwelcome advances he makes towards her young adolescent daughters. She confided to Faith that she had contemplated many times

33

reporting Pappi to the authorities, but because he was a struggling foreigner like her in America, and she decided not to. At first, Faith was skeptical about the revelations of her new husband, but as time went, on her suspicions grew. She started to notice that Pappi's whereabouts were always elusive, and he would often receive calls from many unknown people, many of whom he claimed to be just female friends. One night as they snuggled on the sofa watching their usual evening TV program Pappi's phone rang, and he had nervously flipped it over so as to not expose the number on the screen. In addition, he pretended that the phone was not ringing as it incessantly vibrated on the sofa next to him. Faith became suspicious and asked why he was ignoring the call. "Why the hell can't you answer your phone?" Faith angrily shouted. Pappi muttered some lame excuse and quickly tried to steer the conversation away from his phone. But months of doubt and unexplained behavior had taken their toll on Faith's confidence and again, she was faced with the reality that she was being cheated on by the man she loved. The storm was brewing, and love was again unleashing its fury on her. She fought back like she always did, by bitterly standing and unleashing the ugliness of her hurt in a thundering of curse words and accusations. Faith knew this storm's effect and damage all too well. She had had to survive it many times in her first marriage and had vowed she would never put herself in a situation to face it again. Pappi knew she was mad, and he tried to calm her fears. He inched closer to her on the little beige sofa and propped his short arms around her shoulder forcibly dragging her into his embrace. He uttered in his limited English, "You know I love you, I never hurt you." Yet, words like these were meaningless to Faith as she had heard it all before with no true meaning to them. She hastily pushed his hands away and continued in her battle of words about his infidelity. She could feel her head pounding; her heart racing and the heat of anger had gotten the best of her. It seemed like years of pain and hurt were resurfacing as well. The beginning of this relationship was nothing like her past ones. This was a man who had been her trusted friend at first, or so she thought. Someone with whom she had shared all her past disappointments and trust issues. Pappi had sworn to her that he would never hurt or disrespect a woman. They had so much in common and Faith thought that her fears about love could finally be laid to rest with this husband. She had seen herself growing old with him. He was not her true love, but she did love him. They had shared a love of cooking and entertaining which was supposed to lead to them building their dream restaurant together someday. Their future had looked bright and promising. But love can be unpredictable, and one can never know when the warmth of its embrace will capture one's heart or destroy it. So, as she stood once more to face the storm, Faith realized that its devasting outcome would largely depend on her reaction. She could lash out and then run to cower in fear and hurt. Or she could stand up in bravery and be pummeled by its truth and face the devastating effects with hope and trudge on.

Faith and her new husband failed in their marriage. Sadly, they had separated twice and had tried to fix the marriage, but it was futile. Perhaps it was their almost twenty-year age difference, or maybe being from two different cultures. But only a love that is strong seems to last and survive the test of time and can it traverse beyond age or culture. Many years later, Faith called her girls to tell them of the separation and most of all, the sad news that Pappi returned home to Venezuela. About a year or two after returning home, Pappi was diagnosed with a brain tumor that was terminal. He had surgery but was never well after and later succumbed to being bedridden and died of sepsis. Faith had also called her daughters immediately with the sad news, as they were essentially her closest support system. When Josie got the call from her mom, she only heard the soft muffled choking of tears as the very hoarse, raspy voice of Faith relayed the news of Pappi's death. In that moment, Josie could feel the pain of her mother. It was as if this loss had crushed her mother's hope of ever finding love again.

After all, she was far older than Pappi and there is no way she ever thought she would have outlived him. But the thunderstorms of love can take on different forms. The devastation left in its path can sometimes leave nothing in its place. Sometimes there is an emptiness that remains, and it never goes away. As Faith sadly relayed to Josie the details of the future plans and dreams, they had made, her emptiness was stark and brutal. She explained that they had stayed in touch after his return to Venezuela and they were in the middle of a reconciliation. She had anticipated that her stormy days of love were over, and that somehow, this love affair was going to last and once again lead to beautiful sunshine. She had hope that this second marriage was her forever marriage and she was on the road to lasting love and happiness. It was as if she was seeing a rainbow after her thunderstorms, but life had other plans for her. "He was never sick, he would sometimes complain of headaches now and then, but I had no clue," she rattled on to her daughter. Even through the phone, Josie could sense the guilt and disappointment her mother was battling. She went to say, "He had some strange obsession with certain things that I later learned are signs of people with brain tumors, but I never would have believed he was sick in any way." For Faith, it was as if this storm cleared her heart of every emotion associated with love. She had then decided to focus her life on her children and grandchildren. She had signed off from love forever. It was as if she had locked her heart in her own little fortress, never to be devastated by love's storms again. Despite the occasional push in the direction of seeking companionship, she stood firm. She had stood and faced the storms of love. She had survived and was taking every precaution to stay out of the path of love's storms. Faith never opened her heart to love again.

CHAPTER FOUR

Faith

Rainbows Show Up After a Storm

Love for a woman can be just as devastating when it involves the love of a father. A girl needs a father, or some father figure to teach her what the love of a man is. In some ways there is a void that can only be fulfilled by such a man. Faith was no different. She had accepted the fact that she didn't have her father show up for her, but she wanted different for her girls. Like Leo, her father was a tall handsome man with striking features. Perhaps that was one of her natural gravitations towards Leo. Her father had a presence that was hard to ignore. His trademark rubber boots, tucked in checkered shirts and jeans seem to have been his favorite clothing. At least Faith could never recall seeing him in anything else. He had lived in a remote village outside the town of Sea Grape, so Faith would only occasionally see him at the local Saturday morning market, when he would be selling his produce from his farm. He was a man of very few words. Despite many efforts over the years, Faith could never connect with him. Even as an adult, her attempts were futile. A girl wants to know that she is accepted and loved by her father, but for Faith, this was never going to be her reality. Yet, she had hope that things with Leo would turn out differently. After all, he had been raised in a traditional family and his own father was the epitome of what a dad should be. "Grand Dad," as he was fondly called, was a devoted family man. He was not only loved by his family, but also by the townsfolk as well. But somehow, Leo was nothing like his father; in fact, one could say he was the complete opposite. Faith had hope for the same kind of father as Grand Dad was for her children, but sadly she had the same reality repeating itself in the lives of her daughters.

Perhaps, this was the missing link that had tortured Faith throughout her life. Because not only did her father merely acknowledge her, but her mother had also given her away to her grandmother when she was only three years old. Faith had often recalled the story of her adoption to her children and each time, she would always end up distraught and in tears. The hurt of being neglected by both parents seemed to have haunted her. It was as if she spent her life trying to be loved. She tried to find love in men, in friends, her children, her family, adopted children and anyone who would welcome her. Faith was an easy person to love. In fact, almost everyone in the small town of Sea Grape would often speak fondly of her. But the hole in her heart never healed. All the love of those people and that entire town could not fill the void. She kept reaching out for love, more love, any love. Hence, she had earned the nickname, "Mother Theresa" from Leo and her close family and friends. The irony for women like Faith is that no amount of love would suffice, since the people you most desperately need it from, your parents, could not give it to you. Children learn to love at first from their parents. When that love is not given, love seems to evade one their entire life. It is as if it sets you up for failure in love. Even when love comes in at any point in your life, it's hard to recognize or embrace it since you were never acquainted with it as a child. How do you give or return love to someone, a stranger, when you were never given it in the first place? Faith's parents had in turned both grown up with their own issues of dysfunction; they in turn passed the damage on to her, and so the cycle continued. Faith was a good mother. She gave the best of herself and what she had to her children. She had tried to love her children with all she had. She wanted different for them. In fact, she wanted the best for whichever child came into her life. Over the years, she had inherited many "adopted sons" from the many boys who were friends with her sons. It was always boys, since the women and girls were expected to stay at home and would seldomly be allowed to visit the home of a stranger, unless they were related in some way. Hence, it was always the boys who hung around and eventually became part of her large family. But her biological children needed their father. He was there physically, but more like some "phantom" that would make brief appearances in and out of their lives and not always in a good way. Faith's children never knew their father. It was as if, like their mother, they would never know the love of a father.

For Josie and her sisters, they had long accepted that Leo was a father, but would never be the "daddy" they longed for and needed. Whenever a girl is not blessed with the love of her father, it is as if she too will have a hole in her heart that is ever-present. If she is lucky, she may find a partner that will love her enough to mend that hole. But below the surface, the pit remains, and every heartbreak tears into the mend and the hole becomes exposed and with it many pains.

Leo went on to have four other children in his other two marriages after Faith. Three daughters and a son. But it wasn't until his youngest daughter, Jenna, was born that he somehow had managed to perfect his paternal instincts. This last child was Leo's pride and joy. To see his interactions with her, one would never assume that he had eleven other children. He doted on her, and he was the epitome of every little girl's dream daddy. "Mi bebe," he would often lovingly call to her with sweet gestures of hugs and kisses. In later years, as they would all gather as a family, the difference in his relationship with Jenna and the older daughters was clear. The older sisters would watch with amazement and hurt during these interactions between Leo and Jenna. Somehow each one questioning, silently, what made them not deserving of the same gestures and outward pouring of love. The sisters would often discuss this topic at length, and eventually each would tearfully recount her own grief at not having the father she had longed for or felt she deserved. But Leo was oblivious to the fact that he treated his youngest daughter differently. He had called her every day. Even just talking about her would bring a grin or smile to his now-weathered face. Clearly, Leo had it in him to be a father, and a good one at that. Over the years he had also somehow mellowed out. He was able to be on speaking terms now with all his children. It was as if the past was boxed away. The man these women were now getting to know was different from the father they knew growing up as children. Josie and her sisters were now able to hold conversations with him as a male adult, who was family but in essence, not a father. Even more so with time, never as their dad, but more as that of an adult friend who warranted respect and just so happened to be their father.

Forgiveness had changed the dynamics of relationships over the years. Or perhaps, time was able to heal the brokenness of these women who could now accept this father figure in their lives. He was never called "dad" or "daddy" by his daughters or other children, except for Jenna and his youngest son. He was simply always called by his first name. Reconciliation could not change that. The women, as adults, tried not to focus on the past of living through an abusive marriage with their father. The focus was on the brightness of a rainbow that had emerged after the storm. This rainbow arose as forgiveness forged forward. The dark clouds of neglect had still stayed close in the distance, but the sun was starting to shine through. There was hope for some kind of healing. There would never be a daddy to love them the way they needed, but maybe this man could become a trusted male friend. They had begun the journey of healing and how far it took them depended largely on how much Leo was now willing to be there for them. Through it all, Faith's love was there and was extended even to Monica, their half-sister. Because of Faith's enduring love, they somehow had never really felt the pelting rainstorm of parental abandonment, since Faith's love was enough to shelter them through it all.

CHAPTER FIVE

Josie

One Thunderstorm Can Follow Another

L ove doesn't always come with a warning. Its presence can come when we least expect, or at a time in our lives when we may have simply signed off on it ever coming our way. Josie was always careful in her love and relationships with men, or so she thought. So, when she first fell in love at the ripe old age of twenty-eight, she was shocked that there was indeed a Mr. Right out there for her. She was often told that she was a pretty girl, and with her talent and ambition, she never imagined that finding a life partner was going to be such a challenge. Over the years, it seemed as if she was destined to remain single. Her girly notions of ever finding a man that met all her criteria were killed by the years of countless dates with men who never could meet even the first three criteria on her list. So, when Sam first came into her life, she could only envision him as one of her suitors whom she thought could eventually become a friend. Sam was her older sister's high school classmate so; Josie knew him even as a child growing up in the same small town of Sea Grape. She had never thought of him as a love interest, but her older sister, Destiny, had reintroduced them and coached Josie on his endless good qualities that would have made him a suitable husband. Sam was a skinny, dark-skinned man whose lanky physique reminded Josie somewhat of her father's. He had the same thick, wavy, black hair and his sharp chiseled face was indeed striking. But despite his handsome face, there was something awkward and boyish about him that immediately put him in the friend zone as far as Josie was concerned. She thought he was fun to be around, but somehow, because of his never-ending joking, she couldn't take him seriously. Yet, life has a way of unraveling that can skew one's imagination.

A year after this most unlikely suitor came calling, Josie was moving to Florida to further her relationship with him, to start nursing school, and to embark on one of the most committed relationship choices she had ever made in her life. Sam's love and devotion to her had eventually won her over. Josie had many suitors, but none had pursued her the way that Sam did. One evening after her usual long days of babysitting and getting off the train from her forty-five-minute commute, she got the most extravagant, surprise at home. That evening she had sluggishly entered the apartment she shared with her mother and younger sister to find the most amazing bouquet of her favorite white roses. Her mother had rushed to the door with excitement and the biggest grin on her face to show Josie the flowers. "That man really loves you," Faith said as Josie stood in disbelief gawking at the very huge arrangement of the most beautiful long-stemmed white roses. Her birthday was the following day and not only had Sam sent the twenty-eight roses to match her age, but he had also sent her the most romantic poem Josie had ever gotten from anyone. Sam's lavish gifts, kind gestures and loving words eventually melted Josie's heart. She fell in love with him, and she had fallen hard.

This love had led her to a new life and new adventures in Florida, as she and Sam had eventually moved in together as a couple. Sam had made many promises and even offered to support her fully as she continued her education and pursued her career. These promises were the answer to

Josie's prayers, and she was then certain that Sam's intentions were genuine. It was as if "Prince Charming" had finally come to rescue her from a life of struggling. But the fairytale soon came to a screeching halt, shortly after they had moved in together. A few months after living together, Sam's kind persona was gradually changing into a callous and sometimes mean demeanor. He started to shout at her, or would completely ignore her at times, behaviors that Josie had never experienced from him before moving in with him. Perhaps, Sam' s delusions of what this amazing woman had come to an abrupt halt as well when he discovered that reality was different from his dreams. Josie may have been his dream girl on the outside, but inside she was a broken woman, especially in the arena of love. Josie had tried to share her past and her brokenness that started with her father's neglect, an uncle's abuse as a child and the past that made her the woman she was today. But Sam had come from a family of dysfunction as well. He too had a very unconventional childhood; he had his own baggage. In fact, he himself had never had a serious relationship, and Josie was only his second girlfriend. The relationship had gradually taken on a new vibe as the winds of disappointment blew their way. Their love was suddenly changing, and a new storm was developing that was going to change things forever. Josie was no longer his dream girl and it was as if he had kicked her off the imaginary pedestal he had once placed her on. This did not make sense to Josie at first, after all, he was her "Prince Charming," the man who would not only marry her and give her the loving family she wanted, but also help to heal her brokenness. But Sam could never fulfill these dreams. He had his own demons from the past that changed the course of his intentions the moment he saw that his dream girl had flaws.

As women, we thrive on love's sweet nectar. However, as a relationship evolves, the nectar seems to dry up and we are often left with only the residue of bitter disappointment. A woman will give her all to the man she loves, but when she feels the love is not duly returned, she gives up trying.

Such was the case with Josie and Sam. About three years into the relationship, Josie continued to wait in eager anticipation of a marriage proposal. Their relationship was different, but she thought Sam's love was still there and he still wanted a future with her. She thought it was time for her to finally have her family and her happily ever after. "I know he loves me Ma, I just can't understand why he won't marry me," she had said to Faith over and over as she tried to reason out his reluctance towards marriage. However, Sam appeared to have changed his intentions and failed to propose. He gave several excuses for his lack of commitment. "It is only a piece of paper; my parents were never married," he would often say as she tried to plead with him. Josie eventually got tired of waiting and resentment manifested itself into fights which led to a very unhappy union. Many women like Josie know the longing of waiting around for your man to make that commitment. There is something loving about telling a person you are committed to them no matter what you face together as a couple that marriage brings. Maybe for some, its tradition, or spiritual belief or maybe just the happy ending of the fairytale you were sold as a child. It is as if saying my love is not dependent on external factors and I'll sign a legal contract to prove it. The love is not changed by the gaining of ten pounds, for example. Or, if finance is low or health wanes, the love doesn't. This is the essence of why many women desires that legal contract to love no matter what. For Josie this was why she needed Sam to marry her. She needed to know that they could weather any storm together. She needed to know that he would love her the way he did when they first met, even when the love had evolved into a different phase. He would always be there by her side, contractually binding.

However, the long-awaited proposal did finally come on an unexpected afternoon as they cuddled on the couch watching TV. It was perhaps because she was now about six months pregnant with their son. Nonetheless, Josie was grateful that he had now shown his commitment to her and their unborn child. At this point, she had lost all hope of her dream wedding and only wanted the commitment to signify that they were a family before the birth of their son. She was open to whatever Sam wanted to do as far as the wedding. He would often refer to finance as being the issue or delay, but Josie knew that was only an excuse to stall. Sam was a highly paid business executive, in fact, they were both earning enough to afford many of life's pleasures. It seemed as if Sam, like many men who have commitment issues, would continue to find reasons for not doing so instead of simply confessing to commitment phobia. But when pressed with the plans for setting a date and proceeding with the wedding, Sam would get upset. So as not to create more drama and maintain her health while pregnant, Josie would back down and allow Sam to carry on with his futile excuses. At times, Josie thought she could get Sam on board with the right approach. On one such attempt, she decided to surprise Sam with a candlelit dinner of his favorite dish. That evening, Sam walked through the door and as soon as he spotted the candles burning on the table with the special dinner setting, he burst out laughing. "What do you think you are doing?" he asked with laughter, and Josie immediately became embarrassed at her attempt at a romantic evening. She had hoped he would be impressed and perhaps start to see the possibility of life with her as being something worth pushing for. But somehow, this had turned into Sam making fun of her. Josie felt the heat rush to her face, and she tried hard to swallow the knot of hurt and pain that rose to her throat. For her this was more than just Sam laughing at her attempt to be romantic. She somehow felt that he was no longer attracted to her the same way and her loving gestures did not have the same effect on him as they once did. This rejection was deep-seated and somehow the pain that was linked to her father would always surface during these times. It was as if she was not deserving as a woman because as a girl, her father never saw her as deserving either. It is in these times that a woman begins to lose hope. She will start to see a different reality, even if it is not the intention of her man. A woman needs to know that she is loved and appreciated by the man she loves. For Josie, she somehow knew Sam's love for her had changed. Or perhaps his grand gestures in the beginning of their relationship weren't even about love but were merely an infatuation that had now faded with time. Nonetheless, the wedding did materialize a year and a half after their son was born. Even more disappointing was the fact that Sam would only agree to a courthouse wedding and insisted that Josie kept the marriage a secret. He did not want her family, letting the world know as he had put it. As much as it had saddened Josie that it was not her dream wedding; she settled for it and hoped that one day Sam would agree to a real wedding. Sadly, the relationship only got worse after the marriage. Sam's mother got sick with cancer, and he became even more unhappy and withdrawn. Eventually they were sleeping in separate bedrooms. This love was now in the midst of a storm that was pelting Josie with such intensity that she began to feel broken. All the brokenness she felt as a little girl was also starting to surface and compound the pain, she was experiencing in the middle of this love storm. She had to run and take refuge. So, after about a year of married life, Josie asked for a divorce. Divorce was the only refuge she found as Sam refused counseling after one session. There was no fixing a marriage with a partner who had already mentally checked out of the marriage. Sam was quick to comply with the divorce request. In fact, he confessed that he had clearly checked out of the marriage months in advance and the divorce was a welcome solution for him as well.

Despite what she knew about Sam's feelings, Josie had hope for a different outcome. One day in the kitchen while making dinner, Josie had shared her unhappiness with Sam. They had tried counseling once, but after the first session Sam decided that the counselor was biased toward Josie, and he refused to go back. This was a clear indication that Sam had his mind made up. In fact, after that point, he grew even colder in his interactions with Josie. Eventually, Josie moved out, their home was put up for sale and the storm was now in full effect.

Jace, their son was now two years old when they separated. Despite several attempts on Josie's part to reconcile after the separation, Sam vehemently refused. Josie had felt great remorse in the months following their separation. She felt a sticking pain each time their son got shuffled between the two households. This was not the life she wanted for her son. She thought perhaps, if she tried harder and did whatever Sam wanted that their family could survive and Jace would grow up in the family he deserved. "Our son deserves better," she would reason with her now stoic husband. But despite her efforts of pleading, crying and promises, Sam was unyielding in his decision. The divorce was final a year after their separation, under fairly amicable conditions, with shared custody of their son. Josie's dreams of a happy family life had ended. The day of the divorce, she sat in the close confines of her white Toyota and simply bawled her eyes out. She was now sharing an apartment temporarily with her mother and stepfather and that meant there was no private space to grieve other than her vehicle. The warm tears had freely flowed down her hot, flushed face as she tried to muffle the whimpers of her cry, so as not to alert anyone in the parking lot. Her heart ached not only for her lost love, but also for her son. He would have to grow up in a divided household and that meant that he would never learn or see an example of love between a man and a woman. This was something she had promised she would give to her children, since she never got to experience it as a child. Also, Josie was not sure that she would ever love again. In addition, now knowing how Sam felt about marriage and relationships, she wasn't sure that he could mirror it either for their son. Life had changed Josie's heart. It was her first real heartbreak and during that moment of grief she had told herself that she would never love again. She felt that her heart would never be able to heal its broken pieces. And besides the brokenness of being a neglected little girl by her father seems to have gotten even worse. It was as if she would never know the real love of a man.

CHAPTER SIX

Josie

Sunshine of a Wedding Dream

A broken heart can love again. Josie had given up on love, marriage, and family; in fact, she had signed off on everything related to love. After a few failed attempts at dating, she decided that perhaps God had meant for her to remain single. Besides, ten years had passed since her divorce, and she had settled into single life. Her son, family, and traveling were the highlights of her life. There were always moments of loneliness and longing, but they were short-lived. One day at work, everything had changed with a messenger text from an old high school classmate. Deon was one of the nice guys from high school, but somehow, he had never shown any interest in Josie back then, or perhaps he was too shy to approach her, as he later claimed. The question in his text was of a personal interest, he was inquiring about Josie's marital status, kids and the like. Josie's face lit up as she read his message; she was delighted at his now interest in her. There was a grin on her face as she answered his questions. She thought that he could at least be a potential friend, as that was where she would always first put her suitors. She was certain he could at least be someone to fill some of the lonely nights with conversations. Deon had asked immediately if they could talk, and after a brief update on each other they agreed to get caught up later that day.

Later that evening after work, Josie talked to Deon for hours on the phone. They seemed to have made a connection right away. There was something familiar about him and the fact that they shared a past made talking to him easy. Even though they had hardly ever uttered anything much to each other during high school, they knew a lot of people in common and that also made for more familiarity. Plans were soon made for Deon to come visit and catch up with his old classmate. "You are only one state away from me and it would be nice to see you," he had convinced her to meet up. His visit came shortly after on Valentine's Day weekend. Deon had sent a dozen red roses prior to his arrival and this single gesture was the glue that had slowly started to secure the pieces of her broken heart. Of course, Deon's looks had changed since high school. He was nothing like the slim, quiet guy Josie knew from back then. During high school, he was one of the smart guys and very reserved, in fact maybe even a little bit nerdy. He never showed quite as much interest in girls as some of his male counterparts. So, Josie never quite looked at him in a romantic way. Back then he had worn his hair in a curly version of a mullet, which was popular at the time. His striking features would have been considered handsome, but somehow, his low-key personality did not lend to his being noticed much by Josie. Deon was the kind of guy that would easily blend into the crowd. It wasn't until he scored the second highest academic award that Josie finally took note of him at graduation. He was the salutatorian and had to give a speech which then brought him to the forefront at the end of high school. Josie had then taken note and thought he was an intelligent person, but never thought about him after that point. But even then, he was very much isolated in his small group, and she never recalled ever holding a one-on-one conversation with him throughout their four years of high school. They had branched into different vocational areas of study, but even so, they never spoke even during the occasions that the classes all met for weekly assemblies. But Deon had changed drastically since high school.

The first meeting was indeed an opening for Josie, she never thought that a person could change so drastically during their lifetime, and she was intrigued. At, first glance, Josie wasn't even sure she was looking at the same person. His mullet and curls were all gone and were replaced by a low buzz cut. Clearly, a direct effect of his military requirements. Deon was now an officer in the army and clearly was greatly influenced by his career choice. But there was so much more that was different about him; he was unrecognizable from his old high school persona. His physique was now muscular, manly and very tattooed. Deon was now a very noticeable guy, and he knew it. Even his gait was more pronounced. He walked with a certain swag and Josie smiled as he had proudly walked towards her vehicle at the airport. He had worn a tight-fitting shirt and jeans, an outfit that was clearly meant to show off his new physique. Even, his demeanor was clearly more outgoing. He gave Josie a huge grin as he sat beside her in the vehicle and apparently, Josie was not the only one who was shocked at the changes over the years. Deon went on and on about how much different he thought Josie was. Of course, he emphasizes that it was all in a good way. That day, Josie had made sure that she had carefully chosen her outfit and wanted to make sure she was wearing something that flattered her figure. She wore a black shirt and a tight fitting, green cargo slim fit pants. The buttons on her shirt were purposely lower than usual as she wanted "emphasize her assets" as she had jokingly related the meeting to her sister later. Deon was clearly impressed and was not shy about making it clear to Josie. There was an instant physical attraction between the two of them that was strange, given the fact that their past was so different.

Josie had not planned on making a love connection that weekend. But something stirred in her that made it almost impossible for her to resist Deon's charm. It was as if they were just meant to be. She wasn't sure what became of this meeting, but there was chemistry between them. This notion of chemistry was somehow new and exciting to Josie as she did not commonly feel this way with most men, despite their physical attributes. We somehow as women, often mistake this initial chemistry or infatuation as love and this often deceives us. We allow our feelings to dictate how much we give to that individual even when the feelings are not reciprocated in the same manner. It is as if we put on some sort of rose-colored glasses where our vision is often skewed, and we do not see reality. It is only when the storms of love start brewing and pelting that we somehow take off the glasses and face reality. However, we bond via this initial attraction and the real love will only start to grow as we weather the storms together with this person.

Josie was intrigued and had planned to have a memorable weekend with Deon. She had planned to cook him dinner after they did a brief tour of the downtown area of the city. She thought they would sit after dinner and simply talk and catch up on their high school days. Back at home in her apartment, the courtship had begun. As they stood next to each other in the tiny kitchen, cooking, talking and drinking wine, the dynamics slowly started to change from old classmate to new lover. This was no longer two old high school mates getting caught up. This was a man and woman who were now finally getting to know each other, and who were finding out that there was chemistry between them. Deon had offered to help Josie in the meal preparation and his overt personal touches slowly melted the ice that had long encrusted Josie's heart. In her head, Josie tried to hold back her emotions, it was as if she was trying to talk herself out of developing feelings for this man. But the strange thing about love is that when it comes knocking it is hard to resist it. This was the case for Josie. Her usually restrained methodical mind could not overtake the giddiness of her heart. In this case, her heart won.

Josie loved to cook and was frequently told by her family that she was good at it. She had gone all out for this meal, after all, she was not sure what to expect as far as Deon's likes or dislikes. But she wanted to show him that she had many other facets to her than the shy, quiet girl he remembered from high school. They sat relatively close to each other during dinner and somehow the air of attraction that had permeated the space around them made the conversation quite delightful and unforgettable. They had gotten caught up on each other's lives, and Deon made sure he was clear on the fact that he was now single and looking for someone. And as in every courtship of Josie's past, he professed that she was everything he was looking for in a woman. The girl of his dreams. "I wish we had met sooner; you are the type of woman I wanted as the mother of my children," he had said with such conviction that Josie was now trusting his honesty. But somehow, she was a little skeptical as she pondered on the fact that , like all men, he knew right away she was the "perfect woman." Josie had hated when men alluded to this fact, as she knew there was nothing as far as perfection in any woman. This was why Sam had broken her heart and her spirit. Men would put you on a pedestal at first when they are looking at you through the rose-colored glasses only to kick you off the pedestal once those glasses are removed and reality is acknowledged. Josie felt that somehow her history was repeating with Deon.

After dinner, they had meandered over to the sofa and watching a movie but were clearly more engrossed in each other than the movie. Deon had slowly inched over to Josie's side of the couch and with a sheepish grin on his face asked if he could kiss her. This was going a little fast for Josie. She tried to reason in her head that this was only an old classmate she was supposed to be getting reacquainted with and a kiss would not change anything. But somehow her inhibitions were gone as the effect of the wine now slowly engulfed her as she leaned over and their lips locked; what was supposed to have been a peck turned into a full make-out session. That night was the start of a new romance. Even though, Josie had restrained herself for the rest of the visit. There was no denying she was falling for this guy. The dark clouds of her past relationship slowly started to fade into the background as the sunshine of this new love took hold of her and beautiful skies were now forming on her horizon.

Josie was once again bitten by the very potent love bug. A little after a year of long-distance dating, they got engaged and the dream wedding was in the making. Her first engagement and marriage were not done in the typical fashion; but she wanted this one to be different. So, as things started getting serious in their relationship, Josie made it clear to Deon that she wanted a real wedding, with her family and friends there to celebrate. She had no intentions of going to the courthouse again to secure a union. Of course, most little girls have some notion in their head of what they want or imagine for their wedding day. Josie was no different. She often dreamt of saying her vows near the sea, or perhaps on the peak of some mountain, two of her serene, happy places. Deon was happy to oblige her, and he had let her have full reign on the planning. "Just tell me what you want me to help with, I don't care where it happens, I'll just show up," in hindsight, this could have been taken as a lack of commitment on his part. But at the time, Josie chose to believe that he just wanted her to have her day and be happy. The wedding was set to happen in the small seaside town of Sea Grape, where they had grown up, thousands of miles from their current lives.

Sometimes, a woman's instinct is on point and there are always red flags that show up to clue us in on what is upcoming. But as women, we tend to be natural nurturers and we usually want to always see the best in others, despite what logic would suggest. That is why a woman will go to great lengths for the man she loves even when he is not fully engaged. There were several red flags before the wedding, but Josie would tell herself that they were just wedding jitters and Deon would come around once they began their lives together. Perhaps the most obvious was his trying to cancel the wedding weeks before when everyone in the family had tickets and plans to travel thousands of miles to a little town to witness their big day. "How could you even suggest this to me at the last minute?" she had shouted on the phone after he had mentioned the "postponing the wedding." They had continued to a big argument on the phone and Deon's last sentence was that this was a mistake, and they should just cancel everything. Upon hearing those words, Josie immediately hung up the phone and burst into tears. Her sunshine weather was now cloudy and bursting into full thunderstorms. She had at times doubted Deon's readiness to commit at this point in their relationship, but she had never doubted his love. After all, he was giving up a career he loved and was moving to her state to be with her. She felt her face not only wet with tears, but hot with anger as she contemplated what this meant for not only them but the family. Many of whom had already invested so much time and money into making their day possible. Josie had called her mother right away, for she knew if anyone could fix this it would be her mom. Faith had her share of disappointments and challenges in life and somehow, she had gotten through them with a certain resilience that Josie admired. She had never faced this kind of situation and had no clue as to how to begin navigating her way out of it. Faith was the glue that could fix what was broken. She advised Josie to give Deon the time he needed to process things and when he got back in touch, she should be ready to have him either, "Shit or get off the pot (toilet)" as she would often tell her daughters. She had also reminded Josie that Deon was giving up a lot and that she should be patient with him. And so, a day later when Deon had called, they were able to fix things and the dream wedding was now back on.

On a calm evening right before sunset, in the little rustic seaside park, the couple exchanged their vows for a lifetime of commitment. The sea breeze slowly whiffed through the small gathering, as the waves of the

ocean crashed against the shoreline, and their close family and friends witness the union of what appeared to be the perfect couple on a perfect day.

But despite the wedding day being as close to perfection as Josie had
imagined, the aftermath was very different. Sadly, the wedding night was
not as majestic. Josie was awakened to the hoarse, sorrowful groans of her
new husband as he thrashed his muscular arms around almost hitting her
face. She had cautiously inched over to the very edge of the bed to avoid the
deadly force of his huge arms. They had not spent many nights together,
and so this was a new experience. This night was the awakening of a new
reality for Josie as she learned that her Prince Charming was not who she
thought he was. His nightmares had continued, and her dreams were once
again shattered in the wake of a sad new reality. Her husband was diagnosed with PTSD and his personality was greatly affected by this disease.
He could sometimes present as the most kind and docile man, and as if in
an instant he would transform into a mean and heartless beast. Deon had
never disclosed this diagnosis to Josie during their courtship. Even after
his proposal, Josie had asked that they discussed everything or disclosed all
their issues prior to making the serious commitment of marriage. This was
somehow the beginning of the deceit that she had experienced throughout
their marriage. However, by the time all the facts were revealed, Deon and
Josie had already bought their home together and had moved in when he
admitted his illness. Deon had taken an early retirement and literally had
no concrete plans. Despite his uncertainty about the future, Josie thought
that she could make this marriage work. After all, this man had wanted to
commit to her, and he was willingly move to another state to be with her.
She felt that even with Deon's issues, they could get through it together
and make their marriage work. Despite the rain clouds, she was willing to
wait for the sunshine to appear again. There was a rainbow of hope that
made her think this love could somehow endure.

The wedded bliss and fragile hope were short-lived as Josie began to experience the severe mood swings and angry outbursts of Deon's fragile mental and emotional state. Being a strong, independent woman, who was raised in an abusive household meant she was braced for battle. But how do you fight with and still win in love? Their marriage was quickly falling apart, and Josie felt helpless. Deon, like her first husband, did not believe in counseling. In fact, he had blatantly refused to go, and he had been the first to allude to divorce. On the outside, their life seemed picturesque; Deon had looked like the perfect guy, their home was greatly admired, and financially they were both secure, yet she was miserable. In that lovely home, she felt like walking in a minefield not knowing when she would step on something that could have detrimental consequences. Her life may have looked good on the outside, but inside it was filled with meanness and harsh words almost daily. Yet, she continued to hope that somehow, their love for each other would eventually win, and this marriage would last despite their challenges. There were moments of happiness, but they were short-lived as soon as the wrong trigger word or sentence was said. Sometimes, it was just the criticism of the way she had looked on a particular day that would lead to days of torrential arguments. These criticisms often reminded Josie of the way Leo would often comment on Faith's looks. She would instantly be transported back to the childhood of a little girl listening to her mother being put down by the man she loved. In turn, she would lash out in anger defense as if she had to stand of not only for herself, but also for the mother who experience the same, and every woman like her. Sadly, the cycle of dysfunction was now repeating itself in her life. Josie knew in her being that the marriage was doomed, despite her desperate efforts to save it. Like Faith, she felt this was her last chance at love, and somehow, she wanted to hold on to it with every fiber of her being. Perhaps most women do this because we have that maternal instinct where we believe we can fix things or people. Josie prayed and hoped during the year and a half of her unpredictable marriage. But there was no way she could stay with someone who degraded her and was verbally abusive. She was afraid that one day, things would get worse, and the abuse would escalate, and it did. After their first anniversary ended in a fierce argument, Josie knew in her heart that she had to leave. Yet, she stayed even longer hoping that Deon would somehow transform back into the suitor she had first connected with. Her Prince Charming never came back and after almost two years of marriage, they separated, and Josie moved into a little apartment several miles away. The storm had beaten her, she had stood strong in its midst but had left as soon as it was safe to escape.

Nonetheless, absence can make the heart grow fonder. After a few months of separation, Josie and Deon made a brief attempt at reconciliation. They still had for love each other despite the turmoil. They wanted to be together, but somehow their imperfections would always take over and win. Separation was the logical choice for Josie. But she had hoped that their time apart would make Deon realized that he missed her and loved her enough to make their marriage work. However, after their first disagreement Deon insisted everything with Josie was a mistake and she was never the right woman for him. In fact, he made sure she knew that she was one of the worst women he had been with. The irony of this is that he would later confess to just the opposite. Of course, he always recanted this, stating he had merely said those things out of anger. This phenomenon is all too familiar to many women who experience abuse; the notion of where your partner can love you one minute and hate you in the next. Josie knew that things could no longer go back to the way they were. Deon had made several promises after to change and do better, but he finally gave up and filed the divorce. The end of any marriage will always bring sadness and pain no matter the circumstances. Josie had tried her utmost to make this second marriage work, even though it seemed doomed from the start. Even after the divorce Josie did not want to give up on love and somehow, felt she could have saved him. Love makes us do stupid, irrational things, and Josie was no exception.

CHAPTER SEVEN

Josie

Running Back into the Thunderstorm

What is it about love that makes us addicts to this drug? Is it the sweetness of its nectar that we remember even when it changes to bitterness? Even when we have been burned and beaten by it, we keep going back to it, hoping for the return of what was once a sweet experience. This was the case for Josie and Deon. They had tried reconciliation several times, hoping for what was in the beginning to magically reappear. Josie remembers the first call from Deon after the divorce was finalized. His voice had a certain effect on her, of course only when he was being the nice "Dr. Jekyll." It was as if Deon had two persons living inside him and he had a voice for each, "Jekyll" and "Hyde." It was the nice guy that got to Josie each time. He would always start with his confession of how much he had loved and missed her. He would swear that they could be so good together since all the qualities were in place for the making of a great couple. Jekyll was her weakness; he could touch her heart every time. He was the man of her dreams; he knew how to show love and accept love. He would show up and even on her bad days, when he showed up it was like the rainbows had reappeared. If only Deon was this guy alone. If only

Hyde would go away and never show his ugly demonic self ever again. Then and only then, could she fully surrender to this man. But she had to keep her guard up since she could never tell when the vile Mr. Hyde would resurface. Somehow, Josie knew that he was indeed right about where they both were in life. They were stable and the usual things that would break a marriage apart were not the issues for them. They were both financially secure, there was no infidelity, and there was still enough chemistry to sustain their physical needs. Yet, they could not unite on everything else.

One particular evening after the reconciliation dance ensued, Josie stops by his home to pick up an item she had left. She nervously stood at the door ringing the doorbell, even though she knew he had probably already seen her walking up the driveway from his front door camera. Tonight, she certainly did not look her best. Her hair was pulled back and she was wearing her unfaltering work scrubs. He came to the door with a smile; the smile that had first charmed her. There was a certain innocence in his eyes that made you want to believe his every single word. His small dark eyes also held a certain shyness as well, and this was the paradox and mystery of this man. For Josie, he was her pleasure and her pain. Her joy and her sorrow. Her light and her darkness. In her mind she saw him as "Jekyll and Hyde;" it was always a surprise as to which man she would be dealing with. Her breath quickened a little as he grabbed her hand and invited her in. He had seemed so genuinely delighted to see her. He offered her the usual glass of wine and suggested they sit and chat for a little while. The conversation, at first, was that of any two friends trying to get caught up on the missing parts of each other's lives. They spoke of their families and what was currently the highlight of each other's families. Then, as if in a natural gesture, Deon slowly reached for her hand and held it with such gentleness that Josie simply sat and melted into the warmth of his touch. The tender touch of his hands had triggered a warm glow inside and she was somehow taken under the charm of his spell once more. Meanwhile, in her mind, Josie's thoughts when into a flurry of confusion. 'I can't go down this road with him again,' she told herself in her thoughts. 'He is only going to hurt me again, like he does every time; sweet at first then bitter at the end,' she kept repeating in her mind as she took in the series of events that were unfolding in the all too familiar pattern. She was still in love with him, but like most women who are broken by love, she was guarded and had promised herself that she would never go back to this kind of love; a love that had hurt her so deeply. This is the irony of a woman's thinking. The yearning and wanting of a love, despite the hurt that was experienced. Yet, when he leaned over to kiss her softly, she did not resist and so they had begun another saga in their journey of returning to love. This scenario had played out over and over for the last three to four years and would always end with the same results. They would be together for a few months then some horrible argument would lead to separation for a few months and then back together again in a vicious cycle. Deon would eventually resurface as "Mr. Hyde," and his mean hurtful words and actions would send Josie bolting for the door in anger and pain. She would vow in her heart each time that she would not let him do this to her ever again. Yet, the reality was that Josie had, in fact, let Deon back each time and she had accepted someone into her life that she knew would never be able to love her the way she or any woman deserved.

Many women, like Josie, keep going back with no logical explanation of why they do what they do when it comes to love. Somehow, women are the creatures of hope, who will keep hoping for better even when they are being doused in the weathering of the great thunderstorm of love's hurts. Young girls and old women have somehow held on despite what time and experience have taught them. Josie knew of many women like herself, who would keep holding on and were still married. It was often said to her that "marriages are not perfect," yet she knew many that were far from perfect and more like dysfunctional cohabitation. She thought that after her first marriage to Sam, she would do things differently this time. She knew she was compromising far beyond her comfort level because somehow, in her reasoning she felt all her life she had been running from relationships when things got tough. Women do that sometimes, we run when we are hurt. We also come back as soon as the hurt has subsided. But Josie and her sisters were often told that they were "Alpha Females" and perhaps this was the reason they were incapable of accepting abuse in any form. Josie had seen Faith suffer at great lengths with her father. She had vowed she would never allow a man to make her a victim like her mother, and that was why she ran. Women like her will fight and defend for love or against love, when it is necessary or when it feels right. But they will never allow love to break them to a point of no return.

However, after one last attempt at salvaging the relationship, Josie had finally accepted her reality. Deon was a dysfunctional partner, and no amount of love could change that fact. His last text to her was filled with such vile criticism of everything she stood for; his words had cut like a knife. It was after this that Josie knew this couldn't be real genuine love and if it was, it was not the kind she wanted or deserved. Josie had read his last text over and over, feeling her heart squeezed with pain and knowing that this love could never survive.

CHAPTER EIGHT

Gia

A Rainbow Usually Follows a Storm

Gia had the heart of an angel. She was often told that she was like her mother in many ways. She was physically different from Faith, but emotionally they were like identical twins. It seemed as if people knew of their soft hearts and would naturally gravitate to them like a moth to a flame. Love for Gia was somehow always available, but it never had the ending she desired. So much like the stories of her sisters. Her first serious relationship started when she and her older sister had ventured outside the confines of their little town of Sea Grape, to live in the big city. There was no junior college in the small town of Sea Grape, so for someone to further their education, they had to leave the small town for one of the five larger towns in the country, or the main city. The big city was a scary place for two young women to live on their own, but their mother had insisted from early on that her children would receive an education. She especially wanted her girls to make something of themselves; to have a career and not be dependent on a man. Although Faith had provided for her eight children without a college degree, she felt education was the way out. Her life would have turned out differently if she had an education, or so she thought. Thus, she made huge sacrifices to not only send Gia to college, but also Josie, who had now moved back home and was at a point in life where she needed change. Even though Josie had left home right after high school and considered herself an independent adult, she had returned home after six years of adulting. She had worked for years and had helped support her younger siblings along with her older sister, Destiny. But somehow, after years of working, she knew a high school diploma would not suffice for the direction she had planned for her life. When she had proposed to her mother to return home and go back to school, Faith had agreed without hesitation. She wanted her children to have a life that was better than hers. Education was one of the tools she believed would help and so she would always support them in their educational endeavors. Faith, had to not only provided the girls' tuition and school fees, but she also had to provide housing and food for them. This sometimes meant that she had to send small weekly packages of baked goods so the girls could stretch their food money. She was determined to provide for her daughters to have the education she didn't have, and that was, in her mind, the key to them having a better life than her at whatever the cost. Faith was then a small business owner of a grocery store in Sea Grape, she was by no means wealthy, but somehow, she managed to not only provide for the rest of her family, but also somehow educated all her children to whatever level they chose to pursue.

Faith's daughters' new lives in the city were very different from their lives in the small town. Life in the city meant they had freedom; they essentially had full control of their life. This meant their father, Leo, could not disapprove of whichever new boyfriend or friend they had in their lives. For Josie, this opportunity to go back to school was the chance she had chosen to change the course of her life, which at this time, was stagnant. But for Gia, this new life in the city was an opportunity to finally live her life on her own terms. During her first days at school in the city, Gia met the charming Eddie. Eddie was the kind of guy you couldn't help but like. He had a certain charisma that made you want to always have him around. Also, his large dazzling smile would immediately put anyone at ease. It was no wonder Gia was easily drawn to him. At first, he would visit the sisters at the small apartment they shared with a roommate, checking up on them, making sure they were safe in the big city. This was always a welcome visit for the girls, since they completely trusted Eddie. The boy that Josie was dating at the time knew Eddie and this had made for an instant connection. Eddie had his eyes on Gia and slowly, it seemed like his charm won Gia over. Gia would stay up late into the night talking with Eddie long after her older sister had gone to bed. Before long, they were in a relationship and Eddie became like the third stooge in their group. They spent every day together, walking to school, eating, going on trips, and even doing the house chores as Eddie would sometimes help. Gia's older sister Josie thought nothing serious would develop in their teenage relationship, so she hardly paid attention to the long hours Gia and Eddie would spend together. After all, she knew that she was somehow always close by, so what trouble could they possibly get into with her around? "I am going to stick around as a bodyguard for you beautiful women; this city is dangerous," Eddie would often say to the sisters. This was indeed the area of the country with the highest crime rate, so they were grateful for his companionship. It wasn't until later when Gia became pregnant during their second year of junior college that Josie realized that Eddie was more of a hindrance than a help.

Gia was a petite girl with a slender body, and even though she had looked somewhat pale and sick to her sister, Josie just assumed it was from their long hours of sleepless nights studying and poor nutrition as struggling college students. After all, money was limited and so food had to be rationed. Especially since their mother was the sole provider of all their physical and educational needs. The girls would often buy one meal for the day and would split in into both lunch and dinner. On good days, Josie's boyfriend or Eddie would provide an extra lavish meal. Despite it all, they also miraculously managed to share with one of their less fortunate class-mates, who was their regular lunch mate. Life was hard for the girls and their mother during this time, but they knew that it was a worthy goal. Faith would often drill into their heads that, "nothing good comes easy," and so, the hard times were endured with conviction.

One night during one of Eddie's visit, Gia decided to break the news of her pregnancy to her sister, as she knew Josie would, in turn, tell their mother and it would spare her from the dread of that conversation. That night, they had just finished the treat of delicious fried chicken that Eddie had brought over to soften the blow of the news, as he had planned with Gia to break the news to her sister that night. Eddie sat next to the frail-looking Gia with his arms around her as he would often do. This little socializing with Eddie was not unusual in any way, as this was a frequent occurrence in their student life in the city. However, something seemed unsettling about Eddie this night. Josie noted that he kept rubbing his hands together; a fidget maneuver he would often do when he was nervous. He was slightly hunched over on the sofa, his broad muscular shoulders curving as if he was trying to somehow curl inward. He flashed his bright smile with the gold filings dazzling as he shyly told Josie that he and Gia were expect-ing a baby. Josie froze as she heard the news; a flurry of thoughts flooded through her head as she tried to make sense of not only how this could happen, but also how she would explain it to Faith. She could not respond for what seemed like hours to Gia. Then finally, she said what she thought would not only be her worst fear, but what would also fix the problem. Josie thought of herself as a problem solver, to not make things worse, she started to plan with her sister how they would relay the devasting news to their mother and perhaps to suggest Gia returning an extra semester to fin-ish her degree after having the baby. In the end, Faith took the news much better than the girls had imagined. After all, she was also a teenage mother who had dropped out of high school. She had promised to stick with Gia in every way to make sure she got her degree. Faith later went on to care for Gia's son while she was finishing her degree. In the end Faith's love and devotion to her daughters made it possible for both to have finished their degrees. Both sisters went on to become teachers after finishing school, as the job options in the small town of Sea Grape were very limited.

Life for Gia did not immediately follow a path of rainbows. She too, had to weather her own storms. In fact, after their son was born, Eddie gradually left her life and moved to America to live with his biological mother. He had promised to take care of their child and be there for Gia, but in the end, it was Faith who had to step in and fill the void. Over the years, Gia lost touch with Eddie and so her son essentially grew up not knowing his father. Even more tragic was the fact that Eddie died in a car accident several years later. But Gia had moved on and she had already left her first common-law husband, the father of her second son, and was now married to her current husband, Harry. The news of Eddie's passing was sad to her more so because her older son would never know his father now; that was for certain. Eddie had reached out over the years on occasion, but somehow, he was never able to truly connect with his son. Gia had lived for five years with Paul, the father of her second son, but after years of struggling in that relationship, she had left the country in hopes that Paul, would get serious and change his ways. Women like Gia are not desperate, but they will always hold out hope that the next man will be different. Gia was no different than her sisters or most women. It is as if women want to believe there is better, and perhaps that is because good women are truly deserving of better. But like her mother, Gia had endured in the hopes of a better life. In fact, all these women had lived with hope in their relationships for long after they probably should have given up on hope. They somehow felt that if they could just stand and endure the storms of the relationships, that their rainbows would eventually show up. For Gia, her rainbow finally did shine after she had weathered the storms of life with Paul.

Her "sunshine man" was Harry, who was not in Gia's immediate horizon of men. It was a chance meeting while Harry was visiting his family when they met, and they clicked. They knew each other from childhood since both were from the small town of Sea Grape, but to fall in love and later get married was unexpected. For Gia, this was especially daunting since Harry's family did not at first accepted her as a suitable match since she was a single mother raising two young boys. To make the situation even worse was the fact that Harry's uncle was the husband of Josie, meaning there was likely to be more family drama. The family never quite welcomed Josie, and Gia being her sister, meant she was not welcomed either. But true love somehow finds a way to survive even in the most trying situations. Harry was smitten and he made it evident to Gia, for after only a few months of dating, he had proposed. Gia had excitedly relayed the news to her sisters after returning from her first trip to visit Harry. The girls and their mother had gathered for their usual Sunday dinner as they were, at the time, living all in the same area only miles away from each other. Faith was an excellent cook and wherever she lived, her family would benefit from her delicious meals. She would seemingly throw a few ingredients together without measuring or using a recipe and the results were always an amazingly mouth-watering delicacy. The girls loved having their mother living nearby, and so they made it a family ritual to meet whenever they could and share a delicious meal. This Sunday was even more special than the usual gathering since the announcement of Gia's engagement meant there was something special to celebrate.

Gia would happily thrust out her hand to show her diamond ring as each sister walked into the apartment. She would excitedly retell the story of how Harry had already bought the full sets of wedding bands, including his. Faith was always overjoyed to hear of an engagement or an upcoming nuptial; she loved weddings and everything they represent. But this was more special to her because it was her daughter's. The planning went into effect as each sister would give her ideas of what she felt would be a dream day for their sister.

The wedding of Gia and Harry was held on the grounds of one of the area's local hotels. It was mostly family and close friends. Most women dream of what they want their perfect wedding day to be, and Gia was no different. She loved red and so this was the color theme of the day. Harry had stood proudly under the white gazebo, his smile not only radiated happiness, but his eyes also shone with contentment. They were in love, and the air around seemed to emit rays of such love. Gia had slowly walked out of the hotel room towards the gazebo as if floating on air. She had looked like the epitome of any Disney princess in her beautiful, white ballgown and tiara. Her dark black hair was swept up in a stunning nest of curls surrounded by her sparkling tiara. Her gown was very princess-like, and she would have rivaled even Cinderella going to the ball. She was especially glowing on this day, and the smile would not leave her rosy, red lips throughout the ceremony. Gia had her father come especially for her wedding. She ensured that every arrangement was made so Leo could walk her down the pathway to her future husband. Gia had always had a soft spot for her father, Leo. Unlike, her other sisters, she had tried to always stay in touch with him and she would make extensive accommodations to host him whenever he visited the U.S. This occasion was no different. As she walked toward Harry and held his hand, she knew that this connection with this man was different. There was something about Harry's kind eyes and his loving gaze that put her at ease and gave her the reassurance that somehow, they would be able to weather whatever storm life brought their way. The warm air of the evening seemed to have been reflected on their faces, and as they lovingly gazed into each other's eyes and said their vows of a promise of a lifetime together. This union had been a "happily ever after." Gia and Harry remain married and committed to each other. Over the years, they have had to battle through many thunderstorms, but somehow their love endured and grew. They held on to each other as Harry's family would pelt them with many stormy clouds with the intentions of breaking them up, but to no avail. Their rainbow came along with its beautiful sunny days of an enduring love.

CHAPTER NINE

Monica

Weathering Through All Storms

In the wake of loss and destruction, hope can still bring forth renewed life. This time, the blossoms of new love came through the vines of her little sister Monica. Monica, the half-sister of Josie was Leo's child whom he had fathered during an affair he had while married to Faith. That was another part of Faith's life with Leo that included infidelity and much heartache. Leo had numerous affairs while he was married to Faith, but somehow, he did not father any children that Faith knew of. But this affair with Monica's mother not only included him fathering a daughter but it also tragically ended in the death of Monica's mother. The death was unexpected as this was a younger woman. The child was delivered a healthy baby, but the mother suffered post-partum bleeding and because of the limited health resources in the small town of Sea Grape, she became another mortality in the significant number of women who died this way in this small town.

Monica was a tall and strikingly beautiful woman. Like her sisters, she would easily attract male attention. She had the features of her father Leo and was easily identified as part of his clan. The first time Faith saw her as a baby she knew immediately that she was Leo's daughter even before he had confessed that she was his child. Over the years, Monica had always been in her sisters' lives in some form. As a three-year-old, she came to live with Faith and her family briefly as her ailing grandmother, who was her caretaker, got severely ill. Josie could vividly recall this brief period that Monica lived with them because somehow, it came with such turmoil as if the mere presence of the child had riled up some demon in Leo. There would be times when the children would be bunched around the small table eating lunch or dinner when Leo would walk in the house and his presence would bring an immediate change in the atmosphere. It would be as if a dark cloud had suddenly rolled in, and everyone knew there was a storm brewing that would follow shortly after. There was one afternoon at lunch that Leo seemed particularly bothered by Monica's presence. He yelled across the table at her "Stop eating like that, you sound like a cow." This harsh, verbal outburst had sent Monica into a fit of tears. Josie sat, watching in shock and disgust as her tiny, frail sister sobbed inconsolably. Meanwhile, Faith was also at the stove finishing up the sharing of the family meal. She stood and watched in disgust at Leo's behavior. However, Monica's tears seemed to have aggravated Leo even further and Faith interjected that the little girl needed new shoes and instead of being mean to her, he should pay attention to her needs. She had suggested that he should try to make up for the fact that she didn't have a mother and that he was her only parent. As Faith ranted on about Leo's failure to parent Monica, it only enraged Leo more and as if like a lightning bolt he reached across the table and struck Monica with a slap that sent her little body in a swift turn. Faith rushed over to cradle her before she could fall to the floor. But, like always, Leo would strike his blows and then quickly storm off. He roared out of the house as quickly as he had struck and left everything in pain and hurt as he disappeared for the rest of the day. This event was not new to the rest of the children, as they often witnessed similar behavior towards their mother. The perplexing fact about Leo's physical abuse was that it was limited to Faith only. Faith would later relay to her children that perhaps it was because the first time Leo had disciplined their oldest child, Destiny, he had beat her so badly that Faith had warned him that was where she drew the line with his behavior and would not hesitate to go to the police to report him. In the town of Sea Grape, a man beating his wife was not an unusual occurrence; the penalty was hardly ever persecution, but a man abusing his children would carry harsher punishment. So, with the threat, Leo seemed to have stayed away from ever touching any of the children. So, his striking Monica was a shock for everyone. As Faith consoled the child, she promised her that she would never allow Leo to touch her again and she would make sure things got better for her. Monica had gone back to live with her mother's family. A few years later, she ended up in America living with one of Leo's sisters. Two of Leo's sisters had finished raising her until she left high school. Monica's life had many hardships; like her sisters, she had endured a lot of heartbreak in her search to find someone to love her. But in the end, she did find love, she did weather her storms and her rainbow and sunshine eventually showed up.

After a failed first marriage, Monica had moved closer to her sisters, and she seemingly blended into the sisterhood group as if time had not changed anything. She, like them, struggled in her relationships with men through marriages and many failed relationships. It was as if these women attracted all the wrong men. Even the ones who at first appeared to have all the right qualities would somehow end up being total disasters. Their dating histories had made for many laughs and tears as they would gather and shared their experiences. Monica, even being the youngest, had her equal share of relationship drama. But it seemed like she finally got on a path to better weather ahead.

In fact, the storms were clearing up for these women. Destiny was now happy in the first year of her fourth marriage. Gia was also in wedded bliss in her eleventh year of marriage to Harry. Stacey, the youngest of the four sisters was now in a committed relationship with her friend of over ten years. Life had moved on in blissful singleness for Josie after her saga with Deon. Her sister, Monica, was now also at a sweet spot in her love life. After many failed relationships and dating, she had finally met someone she could see a future with. One evening at dinner and celebrations of Monica's nursing school entry, she blurted out her reservations about the new guy she had been dating. These celebrations or get-togethers for the sisters were not only social events but somehow, they were also venues for emotional therapy as they would often share the details of their personal lives with each other. Mark, Monica's new interest was not her usual type, and of course they were currently not "quite together" as she had put it. But Mark had tried to win her back after their most recent separation, and Monica was contemplating getting back with him. This was only after Mark had called her older sister, Destiny, professing his undying love. "I don't know what to do." he had shared with Destiny. Monica confessed to her sisters, "I think he is being flaky, and I don't have time for that. How can you trust a man after he has let you down?" She would voice as her concerns. This was the question all the women had each asked themselves at some point in their lives. However, some had continued to trust while others had simply moved on. But the sisters had all liked Mark and thought he could bring the stability that Monica now needed in her life. "When a man can call your sister and profess that kind of love and commitment, he clearly deserves a second chance, Destiny chimed in. "After all, he said it took him a lot to be able to set aside his *eggggooo*." The sisters all laughed as Destiny tried to imitate Mark's Nigerian accent, and after a heartfelt session of discussion, Monica was convinced that Mark did indeed deserve a second chance. For most women the support of having a group of sister friends whether blood relative or not, is priceless. It is hard for a forward-thinking, intelligent woman to always trust her judgment when it comes to love. These women were no different. The sisters over the years had grown closer and their support of each other was a critical factor in their ability to navigate through the storms of love. There had been countless times when the advice of one another had helped to sustain what would have otherwise been a failed relationship. Women by nature are nurturers and the ability to uplift each other during times of destitution has been crucial to these sisters. Over the years, many other sister friends have joined the group in some way or another. As a woman, to have the ability to be heard and supported is priceless and many of the adopted sisters have also been supported in the times of their own weathering of whatever tornado or storm came their way. The sisters would often joke, "We should write a book, the stories would be amazing, imagine a mom and all her daughters getting married in the same year, one sister being married four times and we could go on and on." They all laughed as they knew that their experiences, even though being somewhat normal, were incredibly unusual, but still some things were commonplace to most women in some way. Monica, even though, being the youngest of this sister group was herself, married before and had her tumultuous share of relationship dramas.

Monica, like Josie, had lived through her own storms of love, marriage, and heartbreak. But she was now in a place of love and was about to marry the man who had changed her life and uplifted her to new successes. Josie's other sisters had also all weathered their storms of love and were now all basking in the beauty and glow that remained after their storms had passed. There is a certain inner beauty that glows from within a woman who is in love and is loved. Monica had the glow. She seems genuinely happy with Mark and after about a year of dating, they had talked about marriage and having a family someday. "He is really serious about us this time." Monica had told her sisters. "I don't think we will do anything big at this time, but we will probably get married soon." And so, the planning for Monica's marriage had begun.

The proposal came soon after and much to the delight of all the other sisters. The family had decided to spend the weekend celebrating Gia's birthday in Texas, but little did everyone know there would be reason for another celebration that weekend with the family as Mark had planned to propose. Now, if you knew this family, you would know engagement and weddings were occasions for much joy and celebrating. Perhaps, it was the idea of a loved one moving into a new phase of life that should supposedly bring much happiness. Marriage was somehow the evidence of love being successful. Or at least this was the thinking that their mother had somehow perpetuated over the years. The men of the family all knew this, or soon learned it and somehow would all eventually have embraced it as well, even if reluctantly at first.

The day before the proposal everyone had danced, swam, and perhaps indulged in a little too much wine. Aunt Greta, Faith's younger sister, was more like a sister to the women. Over the years she had maintain close ties to the sisters and this weekend she was hosting the family in her grand Texan home. Greta was the immigrant success story. She was not only well educated but had essentially broken through the glass ceiling and financially, could afford the good things of life. It was always a good time at Aunt Greta's house and this weekend was no exception. However, it was made more special by the engagement celebration.

The morning had started off with the usual family breakfast, incessant joking, laughter, and many shenanigans. The men were told that they would be serving their women coffee today with much pomp and circumstance. Fortunately for Josie, this was one of her and Deon's "making up times" or attempts at reconciliation, so he had joined the family on the trip, and she had a partner and would not be left out. Being left out of the couple activities never felt good to Josie. Perhaps that was one of the reasons she had tried so hard to make her relationships work. Her Aunt Greta was happily married for about thirty-three years, and somehow, all her sisters were seldomly single for long periods except for Josie. Mark had happily served Monica her cup of coffee with a big, beaming smile and lots of kisses egged on by cheering from the group. However, when it was time for Deon to serve Josie, she could tell he was not only uncomfortable, but this was something he would never do if not for being in this setting and given lots of coaxing. Yet, the fun had continued with much love and celebrating as the preparation for the tea party later that day ensued. During all this prep work, the family found time to walk down to the picturesque gazebo near Aunt Greta's house to have a formal proposal and picture-taking session. Monica and Mark were beaming as they re-enacted the proposal with much cheering from the rest of the family. This was only the beginning of many milestones in the love story of Monica and Mark. The bigger celebration came months later when they had their wedding. The wedding was during the time of the Covid pandemic and so, large gatherings were restricted. So, they had settled on a small, intimate wedding with only close family members.

It was the day after the magical and serene wedding of Monica that the sisters and their aunt were gathered on the porch facing the lake. They had rented out a house where the entire group could get caught up and spend time together as the pandemic did not allow for much public socializing. On the porch, the group had gathered to chat and indulged in some wine. The glistening water of the lake where the ceremony was held beckoned with its calmness like a piece of art in animation. The grey clouds overhead had started to hide the sunshine from view. The raindrops had started to fall as a tiny dusting of liquid, first like tiny streams of water, then gradually forming large pellets. But for those women, thunderstorms were an integral part of their childhood, physically and figuratively. In the small town of Sea Grape, they would have fallen asleep many nights listening to the thumping of raindrops on their zinc roofs. Storms were not feared; they were more of a cleansing. A renewal of some sort, where new life would begin; new growth would sprout from the confines of the earth and life would continue. Today was no different. The women sat with wine and chatted on, with the occasional outburst of body-shaking laughter as old funny memories were shared. At times, there would be silence as they would sit still and quietly allow the feel and noise of the storm to simply take over. Back in the small quiet town of Sea Grape, Faith sat on her front porch as well, watching the dark clouds filling the sky over the blackness of the sea. A dark blanket of rain clouds was about to burst forth with torrential rain in the town of Sea Grape. She too was sipping a glass of her homemade ginger wine. She was contemplating the many storms she had lived through in her lifetime; both physically and emotionally. She thought of her daughters, thousands of miles away; none of whom she could have sheltered from the storms of life and love. But these women had somehow become resilient to life's storms. The women who sat facing the lake were survivors of all kinds of rough weather. Each woman had survived many physical and emotional storms; some roaring thunder and sharp burst of lightning left each of them only in stillness, standing. Somehow the storm did not elicit weakness. These women were strong; these women knew how to stand firm in the face of storms.

CHAPTER TEN

Josie

Standing After the
Storms Have Passed

S omehow in the middle of the heartbreak storm of love, Josie had found peace and calmness. Josie and Deon had broken up again for the countless time, after the Texas engagement trip. Hence, he was never a part of the wedding of Mark and Monica. Singleness was once again Josie's reality. Josie had tried to reconcile with Deon so many times after their separation that she had lost count of the times. But after the last time of reconciliation, Josie decided that perhaps, dating other people would be the best way to move on. Her family and friends would often suggest online dating or some potential suitor. Josie was not sure she was ready for love again. But her mind told her she needed to move on. And so, in came the brief wind puff of one of her suitors, Gavin.

This was an interesting step back into dating and relationships for Josie. Gavin was a friend of a friend, and so she was open to the idea of meeting this new man. On their first blind they were supposed to have met briefly, merely to see if there was a possible love connection. There were several things they had in common, both married twice, both had one child, and more importantly, both shared the same spiritual beliefs; something Josie had never shared with anyone she had previously dated. Gavin had sent a picture prior to their meeting, and he was an attractive man with a very muscular build. By any woman's standards a worthy catch, and so Josie was very much interested. Their first meeting was an immediate disappointment as Josie first noted that he was obviously much older and less physically fit than the picture he had sent. Of course, despite that fact, she ended up going on two dates with Gavin to ensure that she was giving him a fair chance. But somehow, she knew that this was not the man for her and decided that it was best to not pursue anything further with Gavin.

The ghost of Deon had somehow still loomed closely in the distance. She had loved this man and somehow even though her logical mind would tell her that she was wasting her time, her heart refused to let go of him. Loving someone never came easy for Josie. Deon was only the second man she had truly loved and like her first love, she had a hard time letting go. This, of course, is a phenomenon that was common to most people. But for Josie, she felt like she should be more proficient in navigating her feelings. In every aspect of her life, control was much easier to navigate, but love was different. When it came to loving someone, she trod carefully at first and took her time, but once she had fallen in love, her heart would take over. The heart never does what the mind thinks is best. In her mind, Josie would often tell herself she as completely done with Deon. But his presence would always trigger something in her heart that would take over and the heart would then decide how things would transpire. But during the last episode of reconciliation, the nights of crying herself to sleep never came as they once did in the past. This time, her heart already knew what her soul was now projecting. It was only a matter of getting the heart to understand and let go. Some quiet afternoons she would sit in silence, allowing the memories to flood her with a flurry of feelings, sometimes anger, hurt, sadness or even the old love. She would try to keep her mind busy in order to not let her heart have time or space in her life to take over.

She would sit and even write a book in order to purge her feelings to get it all out so to speak. After all, this had worked with her breakup/heartbreak with Sam. The feelings with each heartbreak would somehow also bring back the brokenness of the "little fatherless girl" that she thought was long gone. The old wounds would open back up and somehow the pains would all become meshed together. After her first marriage had failed, writing was one of her solaces. There were several poems she had written as she had struggled with the hurt, she experience after her first love was lost. In the end, standing in a storm of love is never easy. At times, there would be a sudden single line of warm moisture on her cheek as a few tear drops would escape the corners of her eyes. These times became less frequent as her heart spoke less and would slowly allow the mind to take over control.

In the end, time heals every broken heart. As the memories fade into the distant horizon, the hurt seemed to get less painful, and it is as if time acts as some magic eraser that slowly removes the pain and hurt. Lately, the memories were buried and only the calm of her new life took over. She still had some hidden place in her heart for Deon, like she did for Sam. These men had etched a spot that was tattooed permanently. You never forget your first love, or any love for that matter. Time may have erased the pain and hurt, but memories, even when removed from the forefront of thought, would remain buried. Josie had survived love's storms and so had Faith. They had each gotten lessons that had made the survival of life more tolerable. They had learned that even when love fails, there can be hope. The women had all learned this lesson as they each progressed through their own storms.

Faith had used her pain and heartbreak to try and make a difference for all women. When she had come to her senses as she would often allude to, she joined a local women's group that was in the early phase of development. She had joined this group before while she had lived with Leo, as it was dedicated to domestic violence. Of course, with Leo's objection at the time, her participation was limited. But in the end Faith, along with a few of the women had been successful in changing many of the laws for women's rights in the country. WAV(Women Against Violence), as the group was known, made it possible for abusive men to be punished by the law when reports of violence were made. They were also instrumental in changing the law for unmarried women who were considered "common law" wives and would not be eligible for any financial support if their partner had left them. But perhaps even more significant was the platform that this group gave women to have a voice. Knowing that they now had laws to protect them made women more likely to report abuse, since they would have merely been sent back home to work things out with their partner. Faith was proud of her work with this group. In fact, she had also started a "Women Crafting" group where she had trained women to sew, in order to help themselves and their families financially. Faith was now living in Sea Grape, running a small business, helping in women's causes, and indulging in her gardening. She was also passionate about plants and had cultivated a large farm of vegetables and flowers. Faith had settled into this life of singleness and despite coaxing from her daughters, would not budge. She had resolved that this would be her life. It was as if she did not even consider the opposite sex as possible mates. Somehow, she and Leo had remained as acquaintance over the years. He had become sort of a male acquaintance, that happen to also be the father of her eight children. Leo would occasionally stop by to share a meal with Faith. Faith, despite her continued protesting over his unexpected visits would readily serve him up a meal. Faith would recall on Sundays especially he would come by as this was always when the bigger more lavish meal would be cooked. Leo currently had a much younger girlfriend who was merely in her twenties, but somehow, the lure of Faith's cooking would still draw him to come by. This somehow did not quite bother his girlfriend, or maybe it was something he did not disclose to her. The girls would often question Leo on his choice of much younger women who could not suffice for all his needs. But his answer was always given without much thought and somehow always the same nonchalant "They make me feel young." It was as if these women served only one purpose in Leo's life. They somehow were akin to some trophy that he was proud to display and brag about. But Faith continues to feed him despite whichever woman was in his life at the time. The truth was Faith would never turn away anyone who asked for a plate of food. Her children would often joke that she should just open a "Mercy Kitchen." Leo was the man who had put Faith through much pain and suffering in her life and at times, she would still rehash with anger the things he had done to her. But whenever he showed up, she would engage with him as if he was an old friend. It was a strange relationship between these two. It was as if they loved and hated each other at the same time. Over the years after divorcing Faith, Leo had moved on with two failed marriages to much younger women and countless failed relationships. Even though Leo was always with some woman that was usually younger than most of his daughters, Faith was still somehow present in his life. It was almost like Faith maintained some sort of "mother-like" figure in his life. Faith on the other hand, never remarried and never pursued any serious relationship with anyone else after her second husband Pappi died. It was as if she had given up on love. She became sort of a martyr-like figure and seemed to dedicate all her time and energy in service to others. The men in her life had relished this aspect of Faith's personality, including Leo and her sons.

For some of the other women, going through the storms of love had brought them to the sunny side of love. They had now experienced and reveled in the beauty of rainbows that often-followed thunderstorms. Gia, Stacey, Destiny, and Monica were all still in love and they had somehow made their love last even through the bad weather. The women would continue to have little dark clouds pop up occasionally, but these clouds were fleeting and would never last for very long. Most importantly, they would not develop into the raging thunderstorms that would destroy everything in their path. The experiences of the past had somehow enabled them to withstand even if things got a little intense. It is as if once you have weathered one storm, you gain a little strength through each one and are able to survive easier each time. They had all learned lessons of love. They had learned that no matter the storm you faced, with the right partner you can survive and stand in love with that person at your side. But whether standing with someone by your side or alone, each woman had survived. Like all their sisters, friends, and women around the world, they were survivors of love's storms. The challenges and experiences had changed and toughened them each in ways that had enhanced their individual strengths. They had become survivors. All women were survivors that could withstand the storms of love. And so, "she stands in the storms of love."

ACKNOWLEDGEMENT

My big sis Dee, thanks for always believing in me. You have been my greatest cheerleader throughout the writing and publication of this book. Most of all, you have loved and supported me during all the thunderstorms of love. And to my son who is my greatest love and the man who has thought me to love the opposite sex without restrictions. You bring out the best in me and I know true love because of you.